I'VE GOT MY PERIOD. SO WHAT?

CLARA HENRY

I'VE GOT MY PERIOD. SO WHAT?

CLARA HENRY

TRANSLATED BY GUN PENHOAT

Sky Pony Press
New York

TABLE OF CONTENTS

FOREWORD

What I learned about menstruation as a ten-year-old, and why I wanted to write this book in the first place

My period ended the day before yesterday. I used a normal-sized tampon on the last day, even though I really should have used a mini. As a consequence of refusing to venture out into the December cold to buy a box of mini-tampons, I now have a vajayjay as dry as my grandfather's heels. (My grandfather's heels are stark white. Their skin is so dry that it peels and hangs loose in places; if someone were to take a feather and gently touch those heels, big flakes would start falling like some kind of foot dandruff. That's how it feels Down There right now.) It is so itchy. It's a big production to straighten first two nights. I use super-size tampons until my last day, and I have to change them at least every three hours. I once tried a maternity-grade sanitary napkin—one of those things they give to women who've just pushed out a baby and half of their uterus—and I was worry-free for six hours, which easily made that day one the best of my period. PMS makes me anxious, and my period pain is sometimes so bad I can't stand up straight. As if that weren't enough, I suspect I have a tiny, but very real, phobia of blood. I realized this the first time I had to go for a blood test, about a year and a half ago; it ended up as a long blog post

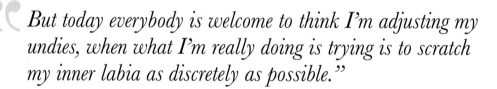

> *But today everybody is welcome to think I'm adjusting my undies, when what I'm really doing is trying is to scratch my inner labia as discretely as possible."*

my panties when it feels like they are making their way up my uterus, but today everybody is welcome to think I'm adjusting my undies, when what I'm really doing is trying to scratch my inner labia as discreetly as possible. All you tampon users out there—you know what I'm talking about.

I began having my period almost eight years ago. Sure, I haven't suffered from intense cramps and PMS (Premenstrual Syndrome)—the kind that makes some of us sob hysterically and spew our guts out—but in many other ways my period is often a nightmare. I bleed for six days, and I always soak through everything, no matter what kind of protection I'm using, during the

(read: a small novel) entirely devoted to the thoughts and feelings my thick, red blood, swishing around in the test tube, roused in me. Just horrible!

But I'm not bitter. At least I haven't thrown up from cramps, which I consider quite an achievement.

I haven't always been the type of person who could talk—at the drop of a hat, without any reservations, to anyone—about the fact that blood comes out of my vagina. While today I may dislike menstruation itself but love periods as a topic, five years ago I flat-out detested them both. Maybe it's Stockholm Syndrome. Menstruation took over my body, and now I love it—or something like that.

WHAT I WAS TAUGHT IN SCHOOL

In 2004, I was in fourth grade, and our educational system believed that fifteen minutes was plenty of time to teach the country's ten-year-old uterus-owners everything about a process they would experience approximately four hundred fifty times over their lifetime.

"This is a sanitary pad," said my primary school teacher, as she held up a flat, lime-green object that looked like a pack of instant noodles. "Soon you will start getting your period, which means that you'll be able to have children and that you will bleed Down There. If you place a pad inside your panties, you won't bleed through your clothes. Always carry a pad in your bag so you're prepared. Any questions? Here's a pamphlet so you can read some more about it. Quit giggling. Time for recess!" And that was that.

There we were, twelve girls in the classroom, not understanding much more than that in a few years blood would be coming out of our privates, and that it was a big secret—so secret, in fact,

that boys weren't allowed to know about it; they were sitting in another classroom rolling condoms down over bananas. Somewhere deep inside my ten-year-old brain I began to wonder why we couldn't learn about both things, but there must have been *something* about the combination of condom + banana that made me happy to sit in the classroom with the rest of the girls and keep a wary eye on the lime-green pack of noodles.

However, as a twenty-year-old, I take offense when I'm told that the lesson has basically remained the same; it makes me want to shout—at least three times in a row—at the top of my lungs, "IT'S NOT FREAKING POSSIBLE!" I hold back so people won't think I have some sort of aggression issue—which I don't think I have. But I really don't understand what brain cell died in the head of the Einstein who decided that guys and girls should be segregated during sex-ed class. I wonder who thought that guys didn't need to know anything about periods. Someone who believes that menstruation is a "girl thing" that ladies should keep to themselves, probably; or someone who has warned uterus-carrying friends repeatedly that of course they can talk about menstruation, but they don't need to make a big deal of it—just take a bloody painkiller and quit whining about it; it can't be *that* hard. Someone like that, that's my guess.

So there we sat, myself and eleven other ten-year-olds, with bodies not quite yet developed, giggling like idiots. I had no idea what I thought was so funny, but I laughed along anyway because the topic had something to do with sex and intimacy, which of course you have to snigger about like your life depends on it. Sometimes I wish other subjects—like,

So, there we sat, our faces beet-red as we were confronted head-on with our future, bleeding, adult selves. At that point, I couldn't make up my mind whether my ten-year-old brain was more mortified by menstruation or by condoms. Menstruation sounded a bit like peeing oneself, except it happened every month and it involved blood. Condoms were like some type of wrapper for people with a penis—at least, that what's they seemed like to me, given my knowledge of things at the time. Each item = super embarrassing! If I had to choose between the two today, I believe condoms would be the most cringe-worthy. Easily. Imagine putting

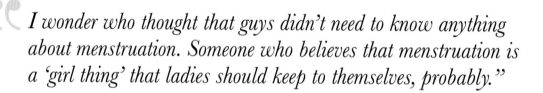

> *I wonder who thought that guys didn't need to know anything about menstruation. Someone who believes that menstruation is a 'girl thing' that ladies should keep to themselves, probably.*"

say, math—had been as big a fuss at school as sex ed. Someone could come rushing in, pale from seeing the teacher prepping for the next lesson through the classroom window, yelling something to the effect of, "HELLO, we're going to have math after recess! MATH! OOOHHHHHH!!!" and then collapse, shrieking with laughter, onto the playground's pothole-filled asphalt. We'd go back to class, look at the multiplication table on the blackboard, and stare with a mixture of fright and delight at 3 x 7 = 21, until it got too embarrassing for our prepubescent brains to handle. Sadly, math is not embarrassing. That's a pity, because it would have made my math lessons way more thrilling.

ten people in a room and supervising them while they roll condoms down over bananas. They'd be scarred for life—there would be no fruit snacks in their future.

IN THE ABSENCE OF MENSTRUAL KNOWLEDGE

This is how the topic was taught in 2004: the girls from the class were gathered into a small classroom. The menstruation bomb was dropped. There were no survivors.

Joking. However, we did wonder what on earth we'd just been subjected to, since none of us understood much of what those fifteen minutes of incredibly awkward talk of "becoming women" was all about. After that, for the rest of elementary school, the subject was never brought up again. By then I was already smart enough to realize that periods weren't very cool; even at ten years old and giggly, I understood that menstruation was humiliating and probably shouldn't be discussed in polite company. Naturally, this made it the only thing I wanted to talk about—but I didn't dare. Hundreds of questions popped up that I never felt free to ask: When will I get my first period? What is it that's bleeding inside me? Does our teacher, Miss Monica, have periods? Does my mom? Probably not, since they've never mentioned anything.

wrote page after page about the different Swedish provinces. However, if Miss Monica had given us a pop quiz on menstruation, I would have had a total meltdown. Honestly. Teachers were about as open on the subject of periods as North Korea is on democracy. If a teacher had sprung a test on us, the overly ambitious nerd in me would have reared up, teary-eyed, blurted out "IT'S NOT FAIR!" (we had just learned those words in English class the day before), dashed home, and watched *The Simpsons*.

I know what you're thinking, those of you reading this who were born in the twenty-first century: If I had so many questions, why didn't I just Google

> *By then I was already smart enough to realize that menstruation wasn't very cool; even at ten years old and giggly, I understood that menstruation was humiliating and probably shouldn't be discussed in polite company. Naturally, this made it the only thing I wanted to talk about—but I didn't dare."*

Hopefully I won't get it either. It would be so great if I didn't get it.

Much of what I stand for—ethics and morals, politics and feminism—I've learned from Twitter. My parents taught me how to behave. Everything else, I've gotten in school. However, I didn't get on Twitter until I was sixteen, and my parents never talked to me about my period, so my basic education in that general area took place at school. I always did well at school—things came easily for me—and I always did my homework. In fourth grade, I learned the multiplication tables by heart, and

them? Well, if you'd asked my mom, she probably would have answered that Google doesn't have all the answers.

She actually said that to me one day when I shouted that I didn't give a crap about our history test, and if I ever needed to know something about the French Revolution I could always Google it. She lost so much of my respect that day. But to be honest, I don't know if Google is the best solution for young students, because when looking at our classroom computer in fourth grade, "dick" always seemed to top "history" when it came to image searches.

Then, totally out of the blue, another thing happened, this time in the seventh grade. Both guys and girls got another glimpse into Narnia's hidden wardrobe, this time slipped into biology class. Biology taught us about the chromosomes XX and XY, and that an egg needed to be fertilized by a sperm, and that if the egg didn't get fertilized it would be discarded by the female. Around this time, someone in class had a stroke of genius and said, out loud, "But that's a period, isn't it?" whereupon half of the classroom of thirteen-year-olds erupted into hormone-driven hilarity. The teacher shrugged, slightly embarrassed, and said, "Yes, that's menstruation."

could be brought on by using tampons. Menstruation was easy peasy—at least, the biological side of it was.

IT TAKES TIME

I'm twenty years old as I write this. And today, for the first time, I found out what menstrual pain actually is. Today. Only now, after having sat through two fifteen-minute lessons about an experience that half the world's population undergoes. After seven years and eighty-five menstrual cycles, not to mention nine sort-of funny YouTube videos, filmed after having gotten pleas for help from nervous teens who look at me as their all-knowing school nurse.

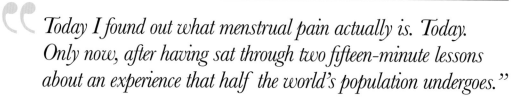

Today I found out what menstrual pain actually is. Today. Only now, after having sat through two fifteen-minute lessons about an experience that half the world's population undergoes."

This lesson came six months after I got my first period. By then I already knew why I was going to bleed out of my vajayjay for six days every month. I'd read the leaflet from fourth grade until it was in shreds. I had it down pat that what came out during my period was the temporary inside lining of my uterus, which had said "buh-bye" because an egg that had traveled from one side of my abdomen to the other had not been fertilized. I knew that sanitary pads were the easiest things in the world to deal with, and even though I hadn't dared try one, I was aware that tampons were available in several sizes. I also knew that I had to be careful because of toxic shock syndrome, which

They worry about their periods; they fret about feeling abnormal or thinking they're dying from some hidden disease. Finally, I know what causes that monthly sensation that someone is nipple twisting my uterus.

My first reaction was fascination. I got this incredible urge to share with everybody why period pain happens, so they could all join me in my big cloud of surprise (and also because I'm a bit of a show-off). My other feeling was disappointment. I felt let down by school, by the internet, and by life. Why was this information not available during that fifteen minutes when we, as ten-year-olds, were made to shake hands with menstruation for the first time? Why weren't we told that most of us would experience monthly cramps that would drive us up the wall, and how to alleviate the discomfort? Not to mention the week preceding our period, when many of us feel tormented by anxiety, anger, and sorrow, without being able to explain why? Who decided not to include this in the lesson? Why did all this knowledge of menstruation, with its accompanying shame and stigma, become something we had to discover and figure out solutions to on our own?

It's because of these questions that today I sit at my computer *writing*, instead of checking YouTube or scrolling through Twitter. I've even gone against my parched genitals' wishes and pulled on a pair of jeans. That's a sacrifice, but someone has to do it, and I'm doing it for you.

Menstruation is my passion, and the fact that all uterus-carriers under the age of fifteen seem to be able to fit their collective knowledge on the topic into an eggcup makes me dizzy, disheartened, and mad. I'm all for lying in bed and plowing through YouTube videos, but I'm just as gung-ho about periods, and that's why I've chosen to totally ignore YouTube today. So, be my guest: within these pages, you'll find everything you'll ever need to know about the subject.

The subject of periods, that is. Everything you need to know about YouTube videos will be the feature of my next project.

Why did knowledge of menstruation, with its accompanying shame and stigma, become something we had to discover and figure out solutions to on our own?"

GETTING YOUR PERIOD

Getting your first period—and tips for rookies and rookies-to-be

Nothing could make me want to go back to the days when I was about twelve years old and wandering around, waiting for my period to start. I remember obsessing about it—so much, at times, that I did Kegel exercises in an effort to squeeze out the menstrual flow, just in case it had gotten stuck somewhere inside. I was terrified I might be among the small percentage of girls I had read about who hadn't gotten their first periods by the time they were seventeen, and who then had to go to the gynecologist to find out what was wrong. I was nervous about getting my period, more

I knew that the onset of menstruation could vary widely between girls—for some it's early, while for others it doesn't start until their late teen years—and that all were equally normal. It just felt that, somehow, it would be my fate to be among the odd ones out—the black sheep who didn't get her period at all. Have I mentioned that I suffer from a slight touch of hypochondria? Well I do, so now you know.

One day in sixth grade, right before class, a guy burst into the classroom. I very much doubt he'll be reading this, but just in case, I won't mention his name to save him from shame. Imagine, if you will, the cool guy, the

---

I was nervous about getting my period, more worried about having to tell my mother about my first period, and absolutely terrified about the possibility that I might not menstruate at all."

---

worried about having to tell my mother about my first period, and absolutely terrified about the possibility that I might not menstruate at all. With dread, I sometimes pictured myself standing there, dressed in black for mourning and with mascara running down my cheeks, in front of all my relatives on my seventeenth birthday, as I explained to my mother that I had never gotten my period—whereupon she and my grandmother (along with the other relatives, lamenting loudly) would throw their arms wildly around my neck and howl shrill cries of despair.

one who enjoys and attracts a lot of attention—you know what I mean. With a sarcastic smirk pasted on his face, he cackled through his breaking, pubescent-boy voice that someone had gotten their period in a stall in the restroom near the lockers. He then rushed out, headed in the direction of the said restroom. To this day, it's still a mystery to me how he knew that someone had "gotten their period" in that specific location, unless he'd gone through the wastepaper basket looking for a sanitary napkin wrapper or something. However, this was the cue for the rest of the guys to let out a grossed-out "Ewww" as they all stampeded like klutzy, testosterone-frenzied hyenas toward that restroom near the lockers to have a look.

So what awaits us when someone has gotten her period in a toilet stall—is blood all over the walls? Is there a sanitary pad lounging in the sink? For a split second I debated whether I should impersonate a guy, throw in my own "Ewww" in a deep masculine voice, and scamper after the boys, pretending to be one of them, so I too could take a peek.

It's with a heavy heart that I report that I will never know what they witnessed in the restroom near the lockers that day, because I stayed behind in class with the girls, all of us rolling our eyes. On the one hand, I'm glad that I didn't run after them, because this would have been social suicide; on the other hand, I could have ended up being the one who never got her period, and then perhaps I would have missed my only opportunity to see vaginal blood close up. Imagine the blow that would have been.

Caught in the middle of this serious dilemma, I felt real disappointment, mostly. All the other girls were already "mature" and had started menstruating, and now even the guys knew what it looked like—the guys who made a big show out of being repulsed by it, making it something to be ridiculed. Personally, I just thought periods were perhaps a bit icky. I didn't have a clue, and yet I wanted to know. It was so unfair.

GOOD THINGS COME TO THOSE WHO WAIT

Of course, I got my period eventually. I was thirteen years old, by which time everybody had already begun menstruating. Not "everybody" as in "everyone else has a cell phone except me" (well, yes, because they did, didn't they, every last one of them—I'm looking at you, Mom and Dad). No, it was more like "everybody" as in "you know, everybody," the way almost everyone seemed to have sprouted breasts and pimples. Sometimes they behaved strangely, like needing to go to the bathroom four times during one boring math lesson. That type of "everybody." But I don't know—maybe these were just my immature assumptions, because I felt like an underdeveloped freak who would never bleed between my legs.

It was on the first day of the new term during the lesson right before lunch, and all I could think about was that my panties felt really sticky. I thought I had come down with some major discharge, so I snuck into a stall in the bathroom to check on things Down There and clean myself up a bit. I went in, locked the door, and pulled down my underpants as my backside hit the cold toilet seat. What I saw made me hold my breath. And no, this is not some kind of clickbait from a gossip rag where the shocker is that I had ripped a seam in my jeans (but admit it, I got a good bit of suspense going there!). What I saw was that my underwear was spotted with warm, wet, and reddish-brown blood.

It's my period, isn't it?

I have no idea.

Nooo.

Yes, thirteen-year-old Clara, stop denying it.

What do I do? How do I do it?

Where can I get some sanitary pads? From the school nurse? From a friend?

I'm going to totally diiiie from embarrassment!

How much will I bleed? How long will I bleed?

Can I put toilet paper in my panties?

Will it work to put toilet paper in my panties?

Do I have any other choice, right now, than putting toilet paper in my panties?

That's it. I'm putting toilet paper in my panties.

> *I looked for the school nurse in my quest for sanitary pads, but clearly she was only on duty between 11:59 a.m. and 12:01 p.m., on odd-numbered weeks and on all days that didn't end in the letter Y."*

Toilet paper in your panties? Don't do it, kids! Substituting toilet paper for sanitary protection is not a great idea. However, it seemed to be the only option I could come up with where I was, locked in that bathroom stall and in full panic mode. As a result, I spent the rest of my day shuffling weirdly, trying to prevent the TP lodged up against my lady parts from rustling. My attempt at discretion can only be described as freaking rough. I looked for the school nurse in my quest for sanitary pads, but clearly she was only on duty between 11:59 a.m. and 12:01 p.m., on odd-numbered weeks and on all days that didn't end in the letter Y. I considered whether I should ask someone—anyone—if they had some sanitary protection I could borrow, but I just chickened out.

Once I had gone back to the bathroom stall about ten times to change out the toilet paper, school was finally over. I went home and began circling my mom like scandal around a politician, hoping that maybe she would just ask me, out of the blue, "By the way, Clara, have you got your period yet?" so that I, surprised, could cheerily reply: "Yes! In fact, it arrived today!" Then we would laugh, hug, and dance around.

My mom never asked. I don't know what she thought of me that day, but if she didn't consider me at least a wee bit irritating, then she's definitely earned the title of Supermom.

A few hours later, my bunched up wad of toilet paper began leaking again, at which point I realized that I would sooner or later have to deliver the Big News. So I told her, "Mom, when I went to the bathroom at school, I discovered blood in my panties." In reply, her eyebrows shot up. What the . . . Come on, mom, give me a break here! "Sooo, I believe I've started my period." She sighed, she said "oh dear," and then we went to the bathroom, where she showed me her private stash of what seemed like a million different sanitary products for different times of the day. Then she gave me a hug and went back to the kitchen, chuckling at the thought of me walking around all day with coarse, itchy toilet paper rubbing against my *punani*. Thanks, Mom, for that boost of self-confidence. You're the best.

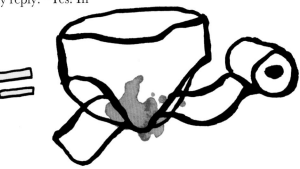

FOR THOSE YOU WHO HAVEN'T YOUR PERIOD YET

It's hard for me to remember what I was like before periods entered my life. I can't really recall what I was like in a general sense when I was younger, but much like I don't remember what it was like not to think about hair growing on my legs, I find it strangely hard to not think about menstruation. I can't even imagine a world where I won't have to wonder "How many days until I get my period again?" Or, "Shoot, my period was due yesterday; I *knew* I was going to

million people who, as you read this, are experiencing cramps or a sore back, or maybe are feeling perfectly fine, or are changing their sanitary products, or have no access to any protection at all. So the probability that those of you reading this are having your period—even though this part is aimed at those who are not yet menstruating—is therefore quite large.

Do you have it?

Be honest. I've been honest with you so far, and I expect the same courtesy in return.

Aha! I thought so.

I haven't got it (either, depending on your answer).

Right this minute, three hundred million uterus-carriers are menstruating. Three hundred million people who, as you read this, are experiencing cramps or a sore back, or maybe are feeling perfectly fine."

---

get knocked up just by making out with that guy last Saturday!" Or, "I wonder if this is period pain, or the fallout from eating that entire tub of Pringles last night?" My whole life revolves in some way or other around my period. I always carry tampons in my bag, just to be safe. Every time I plan to be away from home, whether overnight or for longer, I always check to see if I'm due for my period. During the week of my period, I spend at least five minutes each day going over my schedule to see where and when I can freshen up. And if I don't have my period, someone else will have hers. Right this minute, three hundred million uterus-carriers are menstruating. Three hundred

EXPECTATIONS

If you, dear reader, have not begun having your period yet, I do know how you feel. As tough as it is for me to remember life before menstruation, it is just as hard for you to imagine life as someone who has periods. Well, sure, you probably can imagine it, so that last sentence was unintentionally super condescending. Personally, I truly believed that menstruation would be the hugest thing that would happen to me. It was explained to me as something so grand and exceptional that I could hardly understand how my scrawny little girl's body was going to deal with it. The atmosphere around the subject was so freaking heavy: menstruation was the ultimate sign that you had reached "womanhood," which surely meant that all life's angst was just waiting to befall you. Pain, pain, pain. So how did it really go down, in the end? With some bloodstains and an uncomfortable sanitary pad wedged in my underwear. That's it. Imagine my disappointment.

Still, menstruation is a major step in your life.

On a purely physiological level, menstruation is some drops of blood that come from an internal organ, and they leave the body by way of the easiest and closest orifice. From a psychological perspective, however, menstruation can mean a hundred and one different things simultaneously:

You're growing up.

You're becoming a "woman."

You're taking on more responsibilities.

You're going to binge on chocolate for seven days every month.

You also might become emotionally vulnerable over those same seven days.

Even in this fragile state, you're supposed to keep it together, call in sick, and blame it on a "headache."

These are only some out of many examples. I could keep on writing more, all day. And to those who wondered if I'd have enough material to fill an entire book on the topic? Ha! You must be joking!

Dear Not-Yet-Menstruating, don't worry. I'm well aware that my way of describing periods might scare the crap out of you, and I've done this on purpose. My plan is to make you believe that it's a terrible thing, so that once your period actually arrives you can breathe easy and just get through it without any worries. You can thank me later. C. Henry, PsyD. Over and out.

5 THINGS YOU CAN DO TO PREPARE FOR YOUR FIRST PERIOD

1 LEARN ABOUT SANITARY PROTECTION

Ask someone, or listen real close during the fifteen minutes in school when you're talking about it, or throw yourself into a Google search. If someone in your home uses sanitary pads, get one from their stash and go over its every nook and cranny. Check out all the details. Squeeze the plastic, smell the glue. Actually, don't do that. The glue doesn't have a scent, so that would be a complete waste of time. Try putting one in your underwear and do a test-walk around your house, as you would if you were trying on new shoes and stomping around in circles at the store, a thin sock on one foot and a shoe on the other. It'll be sort of the same because it'll feel weird, unnatural, and a bit uncomfortable, but as soon as you get used to it you won't give it a second thought. Knowing what your options are, and knowing what to do when blood makes its sudden appearance, will make it all a lot easier.

2 SEEK OUT STRANGE ANECDOTES

You can read about how people have soaked through everything over the course of a twelve-hour flight as they ran out of sanitary products; stained their in-laws' mattress; or walked around with blood on their cheek for an entire day without noticing. I have no idea if what I've mentioned has actually ever happened to anyone, but I wouldn't be surprised if it had. Nightmarish anecdotes about menstruation are everywhere. Search the internet, ask your friends who have started their periods, or read the comments on my YouTube videos about menstruation. Try to find the world's bloodiest, most disgusting and foul-smelling stories out there. Once your own period starts, there's no way it can compete with the horrors you'll have read about, and so it'll be as welcome as a cuddly, fluffy kitten.

READ UP ON ENDOMETRIOSIS AND PMS 3

These are two syndromes related to menstruation that I will mention again later. Far from the majority of people suffer from either of them, but if you happen to be one of them, it's good to be familiar with the symptoms from the start, and to know that there's help. Here's your gold star for being prepared. Talk to relatives and see if anyone is living with or has suffered from these syndromes, because both PMS and endometriosis can be passed along genetically.

Don't go on to Google if you're a hypochondriac. Don't. *Stay off Google.* Only one in ten women are afflicted by endometriosis, so it's ridiculous to sit around worrying about something that you've never noticed. Yeah, I'm looking at you—my subconscious. Quit thinking you'll die of cancer when you're twenty-six.

BE PRACTICAL

At the top of my list of tips is: buy yourself a pack of sanitary pads and keep a few of them in your backpack. With pads close at hand, your first period doesn't have to become a nightmare. Spring for a travel-size bottle of nicely scented hand sanitizer, too, because if you have to change your pad in a public restroom there's no guarantee you'll have easy access to a sink; you never know when you might need one. There will be blood.

Also, always keep a bar of milk chocolate—king size, at least—at home. It won't help to prep you for your first period, but it tastes sooo good.

DON'T WISH FOR . . .

Once your period has begun, and strange odors and unscheduled toilet trips become an integral aspect of your life, your highest wish will perhaps be to reach menopause as quickly as freaking possible. Instead, take your time and enjoy the days without cramps, with normal sugar cravings, and with sheets that only get bloodied when you can't quit scratching the acne on your back. Menstruation starts most commonly between twelve and fourteen years of age, but remember that it's just as normal for it to start when you're nine as when you're sixteen. Your period keeps its own schedule.

CLARA'S
MENSTRUATION LEXICON

I so wish that a class on menstruation would become a requirement in school.

Imagine that in grades four through nine, you learn everything about menstruation—from what actually happens inside the body to how periods have been used through the ages as a way to keep women subservient. Unfortunately, biology lessons came the closest to education on this particular topic, and they didn't include any fun homework at all. I'm more of a liberal arts person myself, so it's not surprising that I found biology a bit boring; however, even I would have paid closer attention if the class had covered menstruation.

And I didn't really learn anything about it until I became uncomfortably aware of how little everybody else knows about it, which made me decide to read up and become educated on the matter. When I was thirteen years old and got my first period, I had zero knowledge about what was actually happening to me. It took a long freaking time to build up my expertise, to understand what all the words and terms mean. This is why I have put together a short lexicon for all of you who would like to beef up your vocabulary and get ready for the day when you desperately need to know what a *vampire's teabag* is.

PAD: a flat rectangle with rounded corners that is placed inside the panties to soak up menstrual blood. There are both disposable and reusable pads available. Other terms: blood hanky, diaper.

PERIOD PANTS: an expression of my own devising, for when you bleed through your protection and there are red spots on your jeans.

MENSTRUAL CYCLE: a red tricycle all uterus-carriers are given when their first period arrives. Just kidding. A menstrual cycle is the time between two periods, and it typically lasts around twenty-six to thirty-one days.

MENSTRUAL CUP: a silicone cup that is inserted like a tampon. The blood is collected in the cup, which is then washed out. You can reuse the cup for about ten years. There are no other terms for this cup because the product

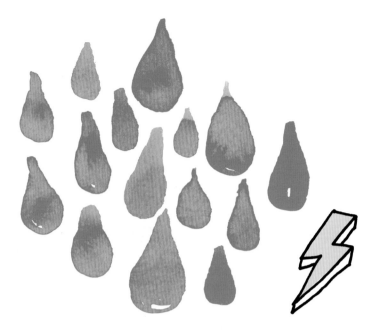

is still quite new, and probably also because it already has a precise and descriptive name.

MENSTRUATION, MENSTRUAL FLOW: the correct terms for periods that only school nurses and my granny tend to use. They come from the Latin word "menstrualis," which means monthly, i.e. something that takes place once per month. Other useful terms are beet salad, red sea, shark week.

PERIOD PAIN: a dull, throbbing pain that can start in the lower abdomen and radiate out through the lower back and thighs. This happens because the uterus is going nuts trying to get the menstrual flow out, and so it starts to cramp.

PMS: what many—but not all—uterus-carriers experience on days prior to their period. It's an acronym that stands for Premenstrual Syndrome, which can mean aching body parts, depression, aggression, and other mood volatility—no one really knows why.

TAMPON: a small torpedo-shaped plug that absorbs the menstrual blood from within the vagina. It's usually about 1½ inches long, and when inserted correctly it goes totally unnoticed; it's removed with an attached string. It can also be useful for stemming a nosebleed, or to lift one's lip out of the way during dental procedures. Other terms: vampire's teabag.

OVULATION: when a tiny egg begins its journey towards the uterus, approximately two weeks before menstruation. The lining of the uterus then starts to thicken so that the egg, if fertilized, has a soft place to nest and grow. It is this thickened lining that is sloughed off and turns into menstrual flow if the egg is not fertilized.

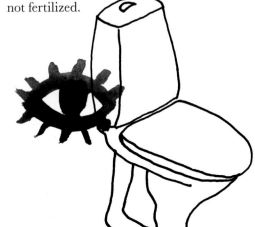

MYTHS ABOUT MENSTRUATION

Now, dear reader, you're almost prepared for your big day. Look at me: when I was thirteen, my knowledge about periods was about as solid as the battery life of an iPhone (in other words, enough to have some fun for a while, and thereafter only for emergencies), but so far I have managed my life pretty well. I haven't drowned in menstrual flow, I have fought back against period pain, and I've come through PMS-induced depressions. Do you realize how ready you are? The first day of your period will be better than all your birthdays put together. With all this know-how early in life, there will be no stopping you in the future. Who knows, you might be a future candidate for prime minister. (If by chance you do become prime minister in about thirty years' time, give me a call so we can do lunch or something. It would be soooo cool if the Swedish prime minister in 2045 had read my book when she was younger. I would get major cred for inviting a prime minister to dinner, to boot.)

But, in closing out the topic of what is good to know before your first period, I thought I should mention a few misconceptions you should dismiss completely. Myths abound, but it seems like the ones about menstruation are as plentiful as *Now That's What I Call Music* CDs—they never, ever end. New ones are released all the time and no one knows who puts them out, but I would like to have a serious word with whoever is responsible.

YOU'LL LOSE YOUR VIRGINITY IF YOU USE A TAMPON!

NO. You lose your virginity when you have sex with someone for the first time. That there might be someone, somewhere, who is turned on by tampons . . . well, that's not in the scope of this book. This myth is sometimes reversed, as in: you can't use a tampon if you're still a virgin. Well, that is not true, because I did, and I'm still alive.

A TAMPON CAN DISAPPEAR UP INTO YOUR BODY!

No—sorry. It's a pity that it can't, too, because it would be so great if the body could just take care of the recycling all on its own. But no, that one is too good to be true. The tampon might travel up a little bit, but it's boringly predictable in its stability; even if it gets pushed in a bit far, there's always the string to get it back in line. And if for some reason the string disappears, you can squat down and use your fingers to go after it. I had to do this once—three seconds of pure panic before I hooked the string and pulled out the stupid thing, which for some reason was positioned horizontally. I have no idea why. I only know that if it really wanted to vanish, then and there was its opportunity to do so. We trust each other much more nowadays.

YOU CAN'T BATHE WHEN YOU HAVE YOUR PERIOD!

Of course you can. You can do almost anything (except: fly, change water into wine, find a cheap apartment in Stockholm, etc.) when you have your period. However, I do advise you not to bathe if you're wearing a sanitary pad. I admit that I haven't tried this myself, but

Myths abound, but it seems like the ones about menstruation are as plentiful as Now That's What I Call Music *CDs—they never, ever end. New ones are released all the time."*

it doesn't take much upstairs to figure out what would happen were thousands of quarts of water to meet an absorbent pad. Even super-plus absorbent pads wouldn't be able to cope. But feel free to bathe as much as you like when you're using a tampon or a menstrual cup. Just make sure that the tampon is fresh or that the cup is emptied, and bathing should be no problem.

YOU CAN'T PLAY SPORTS WHEN YOU HAVE YOUR PERIOD!

Hmmm. That totally depends on the circumstances. If you're about to faint from cramps, it's probably not a good idea to do a fitness test with your class. And it isn't smart to hit the pool if you're wearing a pad. But otherwise you shouldn't have a problem participating in typical gym activities while using internal or external protection. Period

pains are also sometimes alleviated by physical activity, so you should be looking forward to gym class when your period hits.

YOU CAN'T GET PREGNANT WHEN YOU HAVE YOUR PERIOD!

No! Wrong! Warning! Rather: you can't get pregnant if you don't have sex. To make myself clear: *you can become pregnant if you have sex.* And to make myself super freaking crystal clear: you can become pregnant if you have a uterus and you have unprotected sex with someone who has a dick. Over-share much? Take a bow, Clara. Each uterus-carrier is at their most fertile around the time of ovulation, which is about two weeks before their period starts. But the body will occasionally rejigger its menstrual cycle, and if that weren't enough, sperm (those devils) can hang around for about five days, swimming and waiting for an egg to come along. So it may be unusual, but yes, you can absolutely become pregnant when you have your period. So use a condom. Or, to quote from my all-time favorite film, *Mean Girls*: "Don't have sex. Because you will get pregnant. And die."

YOU'RE AT GREATER RISK OF A BEAR OR SHARK ATTACK WHEN YOU HAVE YOUR PERIOD!

This myth is an oldie but a goodie, and yet there is not a shred of evidence that this is fact. True, sharks are attracted to the scent of blood, but they are also

is one headache that has taken up a lot of space in my brainpan over the years—all told, probably an entire hour of deep thought. It's a hard one to wrap my head around, because there are so many ways of looking at the question.

Just as some people enjoy dry-cured ham and others find it disgusting (vegetarians included, natch), opinions on sex while menstruating can vary a great deal. First of all, I want to slay the myth that you can't have sex during your period, because you can. It works great, no matter what gender you're attracted to. Another thing to keep in mind is that no, you don't have to want

And to make myself super freaking crystal clear: you can become pregnant if you have a uterus and you have unprotected sex with someone who has a dick."

attracted to other fresh scents, such as sweat and urine. By the way, how many times have you actually seen a wild bear or a shark? Even if bears and sharks were to become terrifically excited by the scent of menstrual blood, I hardly think they'd track you down where you live and attack you while you sleep.

YOU CAN'T HAVE SEX WHEN YOU HAVE YOUR PERIOD

Well, period sex is possible, since we've just covered the fact that you can become pregnant even when you have your period. But can you really get down when you're menstruating? Won't there be blood everywhere? How do you go about doing it, for real? There are many beliefs about menstruation, but screwing + period

or like it. It is perfectly okay to say that no, you don't want to do it when you have your period. In fact, it's fine to say that you don't want to have sex at any time, on any day of the week, at any hour of the day or night, too, for that matter—and this should never, ever be debated. I hope you are aware of this already, so we can continue our talk about menstruation—because that's what this book is all about.

There have been times when I've met guys who have been open about wanting to sleep with me, while I wasn't at all in the mood because of all the blood that was coming out of my *punani*. In 100 percent of the cases (I haven't been to bed with a lot of guys, but saying 100 percent sounds cooler and more scientific than saying, like, "in three out of three cases") the conversation would proceed like this:

"I don't want to. I have my period."
"Okay . . . but you know—I'm totally fine with it."

Yes, but I'm not fine with it, you moron! At times it's perfectly fine to call people names, such as "dickhead." This is just such a time. Not only because "dickhead" is a funny and very apt word but also because it's not you I'm talking about, of course. I might have cramps, OR I might be bleeding super heavily today, OR my laundry day was the day before yesterday and I just don't feel like washing sheets again, OR maybe I just don't want to have sex because I don't like to do it when I have my period, and that has to be clear. Next time I have this conversation, I'm just gonna tell the guy to go to hell.

On the flip side, if you don't have a problem with it, feel free to have sex when you're on your period. You're not strange—just human. Your sex drive doesn't vanish simply because you're bleeding a bit. Besides, blood is a good lubricant; some experience heightened sensation when they have their period; and orgasms can sometimes alleviate cramping, too. However, here's a quick life hack: make sure you've removed your tampon before you go all the way. But that's enough on that for the time being. HI MOM! Nice to see you've made it this far into the chapter!

In fact it's fine to say that you don't want to have sex at any time, on any day of the week, at any hour of the day or night, too, for that matter—and this should never, ever be debated."

FOR THOSE OF YOU
WHO HAVE JUST STARTED

What?!
It's true?
You just got your period?

Congratulations! Yay! Atta girl, and all that. Welcome to the club; there's already a few of us here—one billion, two-hundred million, to be exact. Some of us only need a few additional visits to the restroom per day, while others are in such pain that they throw up. Most of us use some type of sanitary protection; others are forced to leave their homes and spend their time menstruating in a lonely hovel in the woods. This is probably the weirdest club in the world, considering how greatly our living conditions can vary, but everyone whose vajayjay bleeds every month is welcome to join. Now you're one of us.

First, I promise that you will learn to not give periods even a second thought.

At first it's the most difficult thing in the world. When I began menstruating, I would walk around and check my drawers every half hour, worried that I had bled through. I couldn't quite get my head around the fact that there was a constant flow of blood between my legs, and there really wasn't anything I could do about it except wait it out. It was just too weird. Now it feels as normal as having hair on my head, but you'll never be as conscious of how bizarre it really is as when it first happens to you. You have no idea how often you have to change your pad, what cramps are, how your mood will swing, and what is expected of you. All these questions are always there in the back of your head, like a constant buzzing noise. It's like putting your head in a beehive and trying not to freak out—which presumes you're crazy, or enough of an adrenaline junkie to stick

MENSTRUATING

your head there in the first place. Not that you can compare menstruating to a beehive, either. Okay, bad comparison— just forget it.

I went to bed on the my first night of my period in a T-shirt, pajama shorts, and a pair of boxer shorts, wearing the

that at least I was mature, healthy, and bleeding. Then my period ended after five days. I had forgotten that it wasn't going to just continue till the end of my days. Oops—even though it was nice to know. Imagine the sheer effort if your period was a constant thing.

Now it feels as normal as having hair on my head, but you'll never be as conscious of how bizarre it really is as when it first happens to you."

largest sanitary pad I could find in my mom's stash. I was lying there feeling completely devastated, thinking I would never sleep with the feeling of a fresh breeze on my nether regions again. I fell asleep eventually, exhausted but satisfied

My first period arrived in August 2007. My second period showed up in January 2008. If ever there's a time to talk body panic in this book, it's now. I have no idea what happened, but I had learned—thank heavens—that periods can be super temperamental at the onset, and that it's totally normal if it skips a month. I did start to worry a bit when nothing happened for four months. Not that I dared talk to anybody about it, but my brain held regular conversations with itself in which it loudly and frantically demanded to know if I had somehow, in some way unbeknownst to me, managed to become pregnant. Or if perhaps that first egg had been my one—and therefore my only—chance to have a child.

At this point in time, life's biggest question was: is it better to become pregnant against your will and give birth at thirteen, or to live your entire life knowing that you missed your only chance to ever become pregnant? Option number two seems fairly obvious to me now. You can always adopt, you know. Or have a test tube baby. But when I was thirteen and naïve and panicky, I didn't have a clue. Instead I let the months go by, trying harder and harder with each day that passed to convince myself that maybe it was just as well that my period didn't show up. I wasn't really looking forward to going back to using those nighttime sanitary pads anyway. When my period returned in January, I had convinced myself that the whole business of having children was a total hype.

Is it better to become pregnant against your will and give birth at thirteen, or to live your entire life knowing that you missed your only chance to ever become pregnant?"

AUGUST SEPTEMBER OCTOBER NOVEMBER DECEMBER JANUARY

PERIOD PROTECTION OPTIONS

Here are three things I found super hard to do when I was thirteen years old:

☆ Clear 4¾ feet in the high jump
☆ Spell the word "weird"
☆ Know what type of sanitary protection to use

I finally managed to clear 4¾ feet when I was fourteen. It happened at the regional championship, and after training throughout the entire spring, I placed second. I also learned how to spell "weird" eventually, though I still don't get why the "e" goes before the "i." However, it took me a few years from the arrival of my first period to figure out which protective products to use. Two years passed before I dared unwrap the plastic from a tampon for the first time. By the time I heard about menstrual cups, I was in my third year of senior high. So, if you participate in athletics, you can learn to do the high jump. And if you pay attention during language lessons, you will learn to spell—even the words that make little sense.

And if you have this book in your hands, I will teach you everything you need to know about the different types of sanitary protection products available out there.

GUIDE!

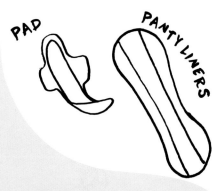

PAD

PANTY LINERS

TAMPON

MENSTRUAL CUP

SANITARY NAPKIN / PAD

Pads have existed forever—for longer than sliced bread, believe it or not. Through the ages, all uterus-carriers have had to put something between their legs to stem the Niagara Falls of blood from gushing out. However, the first sanitary pad as we know it today, i.e. the disposable model found in stores, didn't come around until the 1940s. It was tethered to a ribbon, which was then tied around the waist, because pads with adhesive strips on the bottom weren't on the market until the 1960s. A pad looks a bit like a small diaper, but these day pads come in myriad sizes, shapes, and absorbencies.

ADVANTAGES:

☆ Everyone, i.e. all body types, can use pads.
☆ You don't need to change it every time you go to the bathroom, and it is very easy to notice when a pad needs to be changed (the rule of thumb is: change your pad when you see more red than white).
☆ It is very difficult to spot through a pad if you're in a vertical (upright) position, as the bottom of the pad is covered in plastic, which prevents leakage.
☆ A pad will not irritate your mucous membranes; also, the largest pads can absorb much more than the largest tampons.
☆ In other words, they're perfect for people who have heavy periods, and for overnight when you're not able to change protection as often as during the daytime.

DRAWBACKS:

☆ The blood is collected outside the body, so many tend to feel that pads are cumbersome.

☆ Menstrual blood can emit a bit of an odor, and so pads may start to smell. (NOTE! This does not mean that everyone will suddenly know that you have your period. If someone endowed with an especially sensitive olfactory organ happens to catch a whiff of something they can't quite place, it could just as well be from an unwashed sofa cushion.)

☆ You can't bathe while wearing a pad. I would never condone cutting class, but if you wear a pad you will not be able to go on class trips to the pool. What a pity!

☆ Pads can chafe if you move around a lot. Ouch.

☆ And those who don't sport a clean shave could also have the unpleasant shock of yanking a pube or two off as you pull down your undies when you need to hit the toilet in a hurry. Ouch, ouch, ouch.

FUN FACT ABOUT THE SANITARY PAD:

Most people just to refer to a sanitary pad as a "pad," so imagine the general hilarity when Apple launched its first iPad.

PANTY LINER

A panty liner is more or less the same thing as a pad, but less absorbent. It is flat and thin and is attached to your underwear, and is used to prevent spotting from discharge, or along with a menstrual cup or tampon, or—get ready for a life hack—as you wait for your period when you're not exactly sure when it's due.

ADVANTAGES:

☆ Awesome when you don't bleed a lot, like on the last day of your period. Then you don't have to worry about irritating your lady parts with a dehydrating tampon, and you don't have to waste an entire precious pad if you only bleed a couple of drops.

☆ Great added protection against tampon or cup leakage.

☆ They could save you a lot on underwear if you have bothersome discharge, and you can wear liners every day if you like.

DRAWBACKS:

☆ Panty liners won't work by themselves; you'll need to combine them with something else, which in the long run becomes more expensive than just buying regular, adequate sanitary protection.

☆ Unlike pads, panty liners don't have a side lined with plastic, which means that if you bleed a lot you'll soak through in about two red seconds (ba dum ching).

☆ Many don't even know why we need panty liners at all, and believe that it's just another symptom of our consumer society telling us that we always need to feel "fresh." Because really, when was the last time anyone died from spots of discharge?

☆ Never run a half-marathon while wearing panty liners, unless you wish to have your inner thighs rubbed raw from the chafing. Muscle soreness and knees that won't bend are fun enough as it is.

FUN FACT ABOUT PANTY LINERS:

If you Google "history of panty liners" to find out more about panty liners through the ages, Swedish television celebrity and foodie Edward Blom pops up as the fourth most relevant result. I asked Edward via Twitter what on Earth he was doing there. He answered: "Your guess is as good as mine."

TAMPON

Even tampons go way back in time. Panties weren't always commonly worn, so while some tied knots in rags around the hips to fashion a primitive type of pad, others invented the first tampons. In Egypt tampons were made from soft papyrus, while in ancient Greece linen cloth was wrapped around bits of wood. Tampons come in several sizes, and are inserted by guiding the tampon up into your vagina with a finger. There is a string attached at one end so you can remove the tampon. This string's attachment is more steadfast than a mountain's connection to the Earth. You're more likely to choke on a ballpoint pen than have the string come loose from a tampon.

ADVANTAGES:

☆ As the tampon is nestled inside your body, you won't be able to feel it and it won't smell (one of my most intense mind-melts happened the first time I successfully inserted a tampon. I couldn't even feel the thing in there, and probably stood agape, staring at nothing for a whole minute, in total surprise).

☆ You can shower and bathe when you're wearing a tampon, no problem; you don't have to worry about getting blood on the towel when you dry yourself.

☆ How often you change your tampon will depend on how heavy your period is, but you can feel when it starts to get saturated by pulling on the string. If it slides easily, it's time to change; otherwise you can wear a tampon for up to eight hours.

DRAWBACKS:

☆ Not everyone can or is willing to use tampons, because they must be inserted into the body.

☆ It's not the easiest way to start when you're a rookie menstruator—the first time I tried I couldn't even get the tampon in halfway because it was painful. It requires practice to insert it, to get into position correctly, and to be familiar with your period so you don't end up using tampons that are too large that could dry out your vagina (that might sound like no big deal, but it stings like hell).

☆ Unlike with pads, it's impossible to see when a tampon needs to be changed, which can lead to some spotting when you least expect it. I always use panty liners with tampons, just to be on the safe side.

☆ TSS, or toxic shock syndrome—for which every box of tampons carries a warning—can happen when a tampon is left in too long. But we're talking about a really long time here—as in, days. It can bring on a foul-smelling discharge, which could mean that toxic bacteria are growing inside the pelvic area. Personally, I have never heard of it happening to anybody, but if there's a warning, who am I to tempt fate.

FUN FACTS ABOUT TAMPONS:

 The word *tampon* means "stopper" or "plug" in French. Tampon is a mutation of the old French word *tapon*, which literally means "a piece of cloth to plug a hole." In Finnish, the word *tapon* means "to have killed something," which, of course, can also be very bloody.

MENSTRUAL CUP

Of all the sanitary products you can choose from, the menstrual cup seems to be the thing that people either know everything about, or have never heard of. I myself went from knowing absolutely nothing about it to knowing everything there is to know, all in under fifteen minutes. Someone told me about this small silicone cup, and my mind went *"whaaat?"* while at the same time slowly growing, and then just kabooming. So, the menstrual cup is a cup that you fold up and insert like a tampon; once it's inside you it will unfold by itself. You can order one online or through your pharmacy. There is documentation from the nineteenth century on the use of menstrual cups, but they've never really gone big in the modern marketplace since they're reusable for up to ten years; thus, it's not a cash cow that can fund large advertising campaigns.

If the menstrual cup had an archetype, it would be the environmentally friendly, hippie vegan. You know who I mean.

ADVANTAGES:

☆ If you're a moderate bleeder and use pads or tampons, you'll use approximately 2,500 pieces of protection over a span of ten years. If you're an average bleeder and use a menstrual cup, you'll use 1 cup over ten years. One menstrual cup costs about $37.50. Cheap and eco-friendly go hand-in-hand, skipping merrily towards the sunset through the summer meadows.

☆ It doesn't dry out the vagina's mucous membranes.

☆ You never have to worry about having enough protection, since you always carry your protection with you during your period.

☆ You'll learn how to use a pessary, and what size you'll need. This is the world's most antiquated preventive method, but still useful during certain phases of life.

☆ The menstrual cup looks funny. You know, a bit like a small hat.

DRAWBACKS:

☆ Like with a tampon, not everyone can use a menstrual cup. It is quite large, so you need to practice and have some patience until you get it to fit right, which means you might bloody some panties along the way. When I purchased my menstrual cup the learning curve lasted nine periods, with me always telling myself, "NEXT month it's gonna work!" After those nine months I have come to concede (as I choke up cash), that my body probably isn't designed for the menstrual cup.

☆ $37.50 is an expensive mistake if you buy the wrong size (which I probably did), and in the long run the costs only accrue if you try to find the right size.

☆ The take-out-and-empty process can be quite messy and all-around bad in a restroom without a sink next to the toilets.

FUN FACT ABOUT THE MENSTRUAL CUP:

The cup is known by many monikers around the world: *menstrual cup, moon cup,* or *catamania cup* to name a few. That last term is from the Greek *katamania*, and translates to something akin to "once-a-month cup."

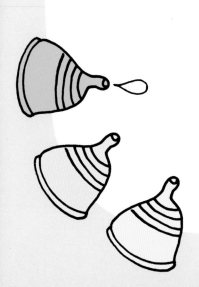

IT'S EXPENSIVE TO BE A UTERUS-CARRIER

The cost of different sanitary products varies widely, depending on what size you need and where you shop. Tampons typically cost 12¢ to 24¢ each, and sanitary napkins run 18¢ to 36¢ apiece. A menstrual cup will set you back about $37.50, but it's a one-time expense. Unless you do what I did, which was buy the wrong size. Avoid doing that. It sucks.

I am a nerd, so I calculated that I, who or "how do I trade in my uterus for something else?" If I had a dick instead of a uterus, I could buy a new MacBook every second for twelve years with the same amount of money my uterus-carrying friends are spending on period protection over the course of their lives.

Unfortunately, the choice of uterus ownership was not ours to make. I'm not complaining about my gender and my gender identity because I'm pretty happy about being a girl, but there is a lack of fairness. I want sanitary protection products to be free of cost. Free is nice. Just like the youth clinic where they give out free condoms.

I am a nerd, so I calculated that I, who use all types of sanitary protection —except the menstrual cup, which I'm going to stop crying over now— purchase twelve boxes of tampons, four boxes of night pads, and three boxes of panty liners every year."

use all types of sanitary protection— except the menstrual cup, which I'm going to stop crying over now—purchase twelve boxes of tampons, four boxes of night pads, and three boxes of panty liners every year. This comes to a total of about $72.00, taking into account that when I did that tabulation I also took the Pill—birth control—to alleviate my PMS-induced anxiety attacks. Adding this expense to sanitary protection, I calculated that I spend about $211.00 per year. Let's say that I will get my period and take the Pill until I'm fifty years old; then in the end I will have spent about $6,950.00 to not leave blood stains wherever I go and to not cry myself to sleep twelve weeks out of the year.

If you're anything like me, you must by now have started thinking along the lines of "shit, it would be freaking cool not to have to pay for all this"

That is freaking nice. I want schools to distribute free sanitary pads.

Sometimes I feel like getting a group of activist-type people together and leading them in a free-sanitary-protection-product protest. I'd put on a pair of old jeans that have seen better days, wait for my period to come, and then go and do everything I've ever dreamt of doing, all without wearing any protection. I'd go to Liseberg amusement park and leave bloodstains on the seats of the Balder rollercoaster, run down the Avenue in Gothenburg with a proud red stain on *meine kleine* ass, and parachute while leaving a vertical strip of dripping blood behind me. There would be blood everywhere, like in a zombie apocalypse, but without the zombies.

I would go on pill strike too, until the pills for alleviating menstrual pain were subsidized. We—my group of period activists and I—would endure our cramps with pride.

I have a very well thought-out, realistic, global analysis of the protest's consequences.

Blood is a challenge to wash out; repeated staining of pants and underwear leads to discoloration, and in the long run increases the need to acquire more clothing. We start having to buy the cheapest threads we can find in order to afford pants. Not only do these buying habits ramp up the demand for child labor in inhumane conditions in cramped dolphins. My solution is that every twenty-year-old who menstruates should be given a menstrual cup or a monthly ration of affordable pads, from either their school or the nearest youth health clinic. Upon showing your student discount card, you'd automatically get 20 percent off birth control pills and anti-cramp medication. Smart? Yes. Difficult? No. So, who's with me?

. . . BUT IT'S FREAKING COOL

Getting my period was incredible, cool, and horrible all rolled into one—not to mention the biggest relief

---

My solution is that every twenty-year-old who menstruates should be given a menstrual cup or a monthly ration of affordable pads, from either their school or the nearest youth health clinic."

---

sweatshops, the women of the West only get poorer. We buy cheap junk food instead of healthy food, in order to afford to continue shopping for new clothes. Tack on increased cravings for chocolate, since our PMS and cramps call out incessantly for more of the neurotransmitter serotonin to make us feel good again. As a consequence, all the added junk food in the diet of uterus-carriers will slowly but surely expand our girth until we all die from obesity-related diseases, and only dick-owners will be left. Since there will be no one left for procreation, the human race will die off and dolphins will get bumped up to the top of the food chain.

Let this be a warning to you, Sweden. I will set this protest in motion if uterus-carriers don't get access to cheaper sanitation products. We all know how it will end—I can already hear the whistles and clicks of power-hungry

I've ever experienced. Incredible, because there's blood gushing out of me without me dying. Cool, because there is mothaflippin' BLOOD pouring out of my COOTCHIE without me DYING. Horrible, because sometimes it's painful, and the whole thing is shrouded in such secrecy. And finally the biggest relief, because it was proof that I was normal after all, which is what my thirteen-year-old self yearned to know more than anything.

To me, my period was evidence that I—with my blotchy red and pimpled face—had the right outfit; even if I wasn't the hottest chick in the schoolyard, I still fit in somehow. Because my interior plumbing worked as it was supposed to. I was bookish and shy, but I belonged anyway, and there and then, that was the only thing that mattered.

MENS-CYCLOPEDIA

So what the heck is menstruation all about?

have always known what menstruation actually means. Totally. Or, what if I'm just messing with you? How would you know? Never mind, let's get to the point.

I like the expression "a bleeding"! That's exactly what menstruation (i.e. your period) is. When someone says the word "bleeding," I picture an elderly man collapsing on the sidewalk. Someone calls for an ambulance and the elderly man is whisked away to the hospital, where the doctors inform us that he has suffered internal bleeding, but he will be all right. I have no idea where this mental image came from. I have absolutely no connection to any

> *I like the expression 'a bleeding'! That's exactly what menstruation (i.e. your period) is. When someone says the word 'bleeding,' I picture an elderly man collapsing on the sidewalk. Someone calls an ambulance."*

SO WHAT THE HECK IS MENSTRUATION?

Here's a list of what I thought menstruation was, as a thirteen-year-old:

RED.

BULKY.

STICKY.

SOMETIMES SMELLS ICKY.

End of list.

internal bleeding except menstruation, and that's why bleeding is my absolute favorite term for it. I survive my internal bleeding each month and I don't require an ambulance. You can call me Superwoman.

I've heard so many stories of young girls freaking out when they get their first period. And who can blame them? If menstruation had not been a *thing*, anyone would have a panic attack at discovering blood in their unmentionables. They would call 911, thinking they were dying. Goodbye, cruel world. See you never.

Thankfully, most Swedes know what menstruation is when it makes its grand debut. We don't think we're going to die

But what is it, this thing that happens? Why do we bleed? Why does it hurt? And, more importantly, why is chocolate so freaking good?"

every time something happens internally which ends in four tablespoons of blood being expelled from the body. I have certainly thought I was dying during some of my most intense cramps, but that's a different story.

But what is it, this thing that happens? Why do we bleed? Why does it hurt? And, more importantly, why is chocolate so freaking good, and so effective at diffusing bad period moods? The answers, my dear period students, lie ahead—as soon as I've gotten myself a piece of mint chocolate.

Whoa, a chocolate craving totally hit me just by mentioning it.

MENSTRUATION

For this to work you'll need a uterus, a couple of ovaries, and a few eggs. Hundreds of thousands of eggs is the norm, but if you're a quick breeder you might get by with a few thousand less. The uterus is a muscle, so if you're a uterus-carrier who's worried about not working out enough, you can take comfort in knowing that you have a rather large muscle in your abdomen that works pretty damn hard every month to push out its contents. Who needs to work out more than once a month anyway? I completed a half-marathon after only having done some light jogging four times over a period of six months. It took three hours, and the next day I couldn't get out of bed on my own, but you see what I'm saying. In other words, this once-a-month abdominal workout is quite ambitious. Who knows, you might even develop a six-pack in a few years.

The eggs live in a place called the ovaries, where they mature until it's time to travel through the fallopian tubes to the uterus. The correct terminology for the eggs is "immature egg cells," and there are approximately 400,000 of them in both ovaries combined. The ovaries are about ¾ to 1¼ inches long until the stage of life called menopause, whereupon they shrink to the size of two almonds. About a week before ovulation, the body's hormones send signals to the ovaries that an egg is needed, and so the egg cells begin to mature. At the time of ovulation, one of these eggs is released from the ovary. Every month about fifteen egg cells start to develop, but only one of them reaches maturation. Occasionally two, sometimes three, or even more eggs mature simultaneously—twins and triplets have to come from somewhere, after all—but that's rarer.

The egg is released into the fallopian tube, whose job it is to move the egg from the ovary to the uterus. Like the project manager my mother raised me to be, I'm thinking that it would no doubt have been more efficient to link the ovary directly to the uterus, but the body was busy fashioning tissue and other things in the way instead, and that's why we have the fallopian tubes. I presume there is a physiological reason for their existence.

It is during this trip down the fallopian tube, between ovary and uterus, that the egg can become fertilized, or—not to mince words—

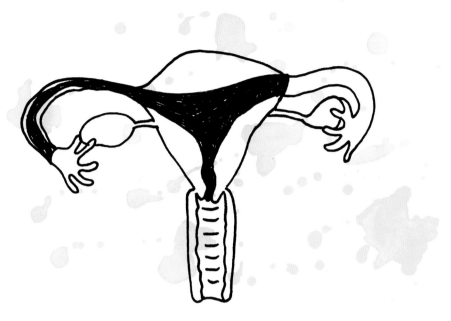

you can get knocked up. I can't say for sure that it's impossible to get pregnant with every mature egg. I haven't gone over *The Guinness Book of Records*, but I wouldn't be surprised if it included an entry on the world's most fertile woman, who's the mother of thirty children. On the other hand, if you don't want

In most cases, though, the egg remains unfertilized, so the body bids adieu to the egg, dissolves it and the lining, and lets it flow out of the most convenient bodily orifice available. And this, ladies and gentlemen, makes up my favorite topic in the world—menstruation! As if you hadn't figured this out by now.

The uterus is a muscle, so if you're a uterus-carrier who's worried about not working out enough, you can take comfort in that you have a rather large muscle in your abdomen that works pretty damn hard."

to have a child for each mature cell (welcome to the club!), your body is decent enough to help you out. When the egg is en route from ovary to uterus, the uterus's lining begins to thicken in order to implant the egg, in case the egg gets fertilized (because it will need a soft spot in the uterus for those nine months it is going to spend in there).

That's it—that's how the menstrual cycle works. It took me years of research to learn about it. I think I'm pretty knowledgeable; I mean, I know a lot of things, such as what an ovary is and what its purpose is. However, I still constantly wonder why part of this sloughing process feels like the uterus is trying to commit hara-kiri.

MY TOP 5 EUPHEMISMS FOR MENSTRUATION

Through the ages the menstrual cycle has never been an appropriate topic of conversation in polite company. We've pretended that we don't bleed at all, and when we've had to mention it, we've invented code words so no outsider would catch on.

But to be perfectly frank, how okay is it to call your period, like, "the red menace"? What about it is so dangerous? Or "a visit from Aunt Flo"? No, if we must use euphemisms, we need to start using good alternatives.

Here's my Top Five . . .

1.
"THE RED LAMP IS LIT"

I heard this one from a girl in my team once, when we were at training camp in Italy. The whole group was walking from the hotel to the stadium, when she suddenly came to a halt, her eyes lit with panic. Someone asked her what was wrong, and she muttered weakly " I . . . it is . . . ahem . . . the red lamp is lit." We immediately understood what she was talking about, even though none of us had ever heard the expression before. It's such an eloquent way of saying it. I love it!

2.
"PARTY WEEK IS HERE"

I read this on someone's website while I was doing research. I don't usually party any more than usual when I have my period, but this euphemism makes me feel pretty happy and more enthusiastic about bleeding between my legs.

3.
"MY LADY PARTS ARE EATING BEET SALAD"

Take a hike, "lingonberry week"! I imagine my labia opening, baring some sharp teeth and devouring a dark-red, lumpy mess of beets from a silver platter. It's a very entertaining, if slightly disgusting, mental picture.

4.
"MY SHARK WEEK"

Not that you run the risk of being eaten by a shark because you're menstruating, but old myths die hard, this one being the inspiration for this euphemism—which, incidentally, is very popular in the US. Granted, it is a bit more badass to say that your bellyache is due to your "shark week" instead of your period!

5.
"I SUFFER FROM INTERNAL BLEEDING"

How cool is it that you survive internal bleeding each month? Exactly. It is "Holy Freaking Crap!" cool.

MENSTRUAL CRAMPS

I remember my first encounter with period cramps very clearly. A couple of my friends and I were waiting in class to go on lunch break. This was the second time I had my period—after that mysterious and frighteningly long pause of several months—and I thought to myself, *Bloody hell, this is going to be major. I'm going to get mad, I'm going to scream, I'm going to crawl on the ground and throw up from these cramps, I'm going to sweat and I'm going to stink. Come on already, Period. I'm ready for you.*

We were standing outside bamba*, and I wondered if I had placed the

Great, I thought. Now the coast was clear. I could be grouchy as all get-out, and my friends would totally understand. The guys could yell: "Why, do you have your peeeeriod?" as much as they wanted, and I would have every right to yell "NOOOO" right back at them and storm out of the place.

I usually relate this episode when I talk about my first experience with period pain. Even taking into consideration my exceedingly inflated expectations, I didn't feel anything more than a weird sensation in my body, and an off feeling in my stomach. It was almost a letdown. Surely it couldn't be that hard to send me some hellish, tornado-like cramps? Just so I'd

> *I've never been on a plane that needed to make an emergency landing, but if that ever happens I'll know exactly how to brace. I'll just have to remember that day on the park bench."*

pad correctly. It felt warm and damp. I felt a dull throbbing in my abdomen, and couldn't decide if it was because of hunger or if it was the alleged and infamous . . . period pain.

"Ouch," I said, attempting to sound as if I were suffering terribly. "My stomach hurts sooo bad."

"Oh no," said one of my girlfriends.

"Hm. I know I'm going to be a bit crabby today. I'm just putting you on notice."

"Okay."

*Gothenburg vernacular for dining hall; a bit of trivia for you.

know what it felt like? "Please abdomen, teach me!" I begged.

A few months later, I bitterly regretted my wish. I had just begun having my period while the whole family was on a holiday trip. What had felt, in the morning, like my uterus trying to turn itself inside out later morphed into the sensation that all the black holes in the universe were centered on a point in my belly, and were all trying to be sucked into themselves. I sat on a park bench, my head in my arms, my surroundings a mere white noise next to the full-scale, extraterrestrial conflict that was taking place below my navel.

I competed in sports for seven years and believe that interval training is the worst kind of torture, but I think I sweated more on that park bench, while bent over at the waist, than I ever did during interval sprints of 8 x 440 yards.

I've never been on a plane that needed to make an emergency landing, but if that ever happens I'll know exactly how to brace. I'll just have to remember that day on the park bench: keep my head between my legs, and disassociate my uterus from my consciousness. *Et voilà.*

No children for me if it's more painful to give birth than to go through period cramps.

Still, nobody ever warned me of this overwhelming feeling that would push me (and my uterus) to beg for the sweet release of death. On the one hand, it makes sense: when you think about most scenarios in which you might lose blood, most of them tend to hurt. Falling and scraping yourself hurts, cutting yourself with a knife is painful, etc. Blood usually equals pain, so it follows that menstruation should hurt, too. On the other hand, there are always exceptions—the nosebleed is an example of painless internal bleeding. Occasionally I'll find bloodstains on my body, and I don't have a clue how or why I'm bleeding; the latter isn't all that reassuring.

Still, nobody ever warned me of this overwhelming feeling that would push me (and my uterus) to beg for the sweet release of death.”

5 ITEMS OF CLOTHING THAT CRAMPY BELLIES LOVE

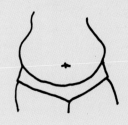

1.
HAREM PANTS

Elastic waistbands are my biggest problem when my belly aches—
regardless of how slack they are, they still dig in to me. I'm sore
everywhere, and the slightest pressure makes me feel like I'm suffering
from five-star exercise soreness. Harem pants have the world's droopiest
crotch, so it doesn't matter if I set the waistband on my hips, or just
below the navel, or at the waist, or even under my breasts—the pants
will still fit perfectly, regardless of location. Yes, please!

2.
ONE-PIECE BODY SUIT

No waistbands to deal with. Problem solved.

3.
FLUFFY SOCKS

Not to sneer at regular socks, but I've realized that it is very satisfying to
feel cozy. I don't know if it's from spending way too much time reading
inspirational Tumblr posts, or if it's an instinct I share with every
modern-day human being. Whatever the reason, I feel so much better
when I look in the mirror and think "I look real comfy." With fluffy
socks on my feet, I get the warm fuzzies.

4.
THICK, EXTRA-LARGE SWEATERS

I usually wear a size small, but I have one thick sweater that could
almost double as a dress. Again, elastic waistbands can be a nuisance,
and a regular, thin dress or a long T-shirt can be too chilly. Putting on
my thick sweater that goes down to my knees (worn together with some
fluffy socks—see above) is such a relief in so many ways.

5.
COMFORTERS

There is nothing better to do the morning you wake up with cramps
than to get up, wrap yourself in a comforter like a hot dog, and not put
anything else on for the rest of the day. This takes into account that
you have the day off, of course, and that you can putter around in your
comforter at home. But who am I to stop you if you insist on going to
school or work dressed only in your comforter?

WHAT IS ACTUALLY HAPPENING?

Menstrual cramps are the result of the uterus pushing out blood. Okay, I believe that, but my analytical self began to wonder why it doesn't hurt, then, when the body pushes out phlegm when we sneeze. Or when we go to the bathroom? Considering how regularly and willingly some people compare periods to poop ("What? We have to talk more about menstruation? Then we may as well talk more about crapping—do you want me to tell you every time I've taken a dump?"), the latter is rather relevant.

giving birth—to an incredibly small baby made of menstrual blood, which your vagina doesn't have to dilate several inches to let out. All things considered, period pain doesn't sound so bad after all.

Have you ever had lactic acid build up in your muscles? You know, like when you're doing sports and you start feeling so tired that all your muscles ache? Or let's say you don't work out, but you still took part in the school's cross-country run—a distance much greater than the one between your couch and your fridge.

Lactic acid buildup happens when one or several muscles work so hard that the circulation of blood can't keep

---

Those are the same contractions that the uterus uses to push out a baby, so if you sometimes feel really horrible during the most intense cramps, imagine that you're giving birth. All things considered, period pain doesn't sound so bad after all. "

There are a lot of differences between Number Two and menstrual flow (I'll come back to that in a bit), but here is one major contrast: We go to the toilet when we need to crap, and in the same way we can keep the crap in, we can also use muscles to push it out. However, the uterus is a muscle that we do not control directly. It knows all by itself when it's time to empty itself, and it does so without us being able to do anything about it. When it is time for a period to begin, the uterus starts contracting in order to slowly but methodically push out the blood. Those are the same contractions that the uterus uses to push out a baby, so if you sometimes feel really horrible during the most intense cramps, imagine that you're

up; the transport of oxygen to the muscles is inadequate for the muscles to work optimally.

For example, you can experience lactic acid buildup in your legs while running, or in your abs during a core workout—or in your uterus during menstruation. Yep, you read that right. Period pain is lactic acid buildup. To make the layer of blood inside the uterus disconnect and vacate the body, the uterus has to work so hard that it runs out of oxygen. This lack of oxygen brings on the cramps, but since the uterus is one stubborn muscle it keeps working anyway. The uterus is the body's equivalent of Sisyphus of Greek mythology. Sisyphus was condemned to keep rolling a boulder uphill, over and over again. Do a Google search on him. I'll bet you all the sanitary products in the world that Sisyphus had ginormous lactic acid buildup.

Almost all women endure some type of period pain in their lifetime. I only experienced it sporadically during the first years, but later, when I was about eighteen, the cramps came down harder than me on a bag of potato chips on a Saturday night. When it was at its worst, the pain in my belly, back, and groin felt like pure torture, and I didn't know where to turn. You've known pain when you've seriously pondered whether it's physically possible to hibernate for a few days.

Not everybody gets cramps, even though they're pretty common. For some, it varies from month to month. Some women bypass period pain completely because all uterus-carriers have different levels of prostaglandins, the hormone-like substances that bring on uterine contractions—the more prostaglandins you have, the harder the uterus works, and the more pain you'll experience. If you who are reading this happen to be one of those lucky devils who never experience period pain, you've been given a reprieve, as well as the right amount of prostaglandin to make your uterus push out the menstrual flow without you going absolutely batshit crazy.

MENSTRUATION GIVES YOU RIGHTS

After only a three-minute internet search, I find out that on this day about seventeen percent of the world's uterus-carriers are menstruating. That means that 334 million people have blood running out of their vaginas, and so feel sweaty; crave sweets; and feel hungry and smelly, or as if their lower body is

trying to pop out of joint. Or perhaps they feel just normal, which is not as interesting to write about, so I think we'll assume that most of the millions are feeling weird in one way or another. During my quick search I also found statistics showing that approximately half of all menstruators have period pain. Half of 334 million equals 167 million. With cramps. Right now. Whoa.

What I think is most difficult to appreciate, when you're in the throes of pain, is that menstruation takes place for the good of mankind. Just like chips. The world is a better place with chips. Without periods, the world would definitely not be as good a place, because we wouldn't exist. None of us. Menstruation is an incredibly big deal with just one purpose. I, along with billions of others, suffer from painful internal bleeding every month to secure the wellbeing and survival of mankind. Join the line for autographs, please.

That's also the perfect justification for you, a uterus-carrier, to expect certain privileges. The people around you have certain obligations. For example, it is your right to have someone you like feed you ice cream. Personally, I like this person be topless, but that's ultimately up to you. Your nearest and dearest are also obliged to hug you just a little bit more, to be understanding when you haven't got the strength to make dinner, and to bring you your favorite candy from the store on the first day of your period. People around you need not feel sorry for you, but it is within your rights to feel sorry for yourself. It's the law. I promise. Look it up.

WALLOWING IN SELF-PITY

Typically there are only two things I think about when I'm lying in bed and trying to distract myself from the feeling that my uterus is being stabbed. One: kittens with fine, fluffy, soft fur and tiny paws; two: "I feel so bad, please let me crawl into a corner for the rest of the week. I'm probably in more pain than anybody in the world right now. I've been taken over by cramps and they are SO PAINFUL, so please give me some attention for once, thanks."

This is the height of my self-pity— I'm bundled in comforters, enjoying free chocolates bought for me by my nearest and dearest, drinking rooibos tea while watching Netflix and feeling a tinge of stomach pain.

I once had severe tonsillitis and wanted to scream in pain every time I swallowed (which I wasn't able to do because, like I said, I had tonsillitis), but my feelings of self-pity at the time were nowhere near what I go through with period pain, which essentially turns me into a four-year-old who has dropped her ice cream. All empathy I might feel for anyone else packs its bags and goes off on a weekend jaunt.

I have this dream about creating menstruation retreats. Imagine that all over the world there are groups that meet twice a week, where anyone suffering from cramps or PMS on that day is welcome to enjoy some raspberry thumbprint cookies, drink coffee, and discuss PMS-induced anxiety and uterus cramping, at the price of $2.50 per vagina for the coffee. Feel free to swipe this business plan—my presence would be a given, naturally. And if no one else wants to develop my brilliant idea, you're all welcome back to my place for menstrual circles every Tuesday and Thursday! I'll go plug in the coffeemaker.

> *Period pain essentially turns me into a four-year-old who has dropped her ice cream. All empathy I might feel for anyone else packs its bags and goes off on a weekend jaunt."*

CLARA'S RASPBERRY THUMBPRINT COOKIES

MAKES ABOUT 20 COOKIES

2 cups all-purpose flour
½ cup sugar
1 tsp baking powder
2 tsp vanilla sugar
⅞ cup butter
½ cup raspberry jam

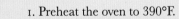

1. Preheat the oven to 390°F.
2. Put flour, sugar, baking powder, and vanilla sugar in a bowl. Mix a little.
3. Cut the butter into pieces and mix them with the dry ingredients until you have dough.
4. Roll the dough into small balls and put them in muffin tins.
5. Push your thumb into each ball and place a blob of raspberry jam in each of the dents.
6. Bake in the oven for about 10 minutes, and your menstrual circle kaffeeklatsch is ready to go.

5

TOP TIPS FOR

OWNING

THE CRAP OUT OF YOUR PAIN

PAIN RELIEVERS

You'd think that, with half of the world's population owning a uterus and most of them menstruating, researchers would have found effective pain relief to take care of cramps. But they haven't. Thanks a bunch, patriarchy! However, there are many over-the-counter medications out there that can soften the pain. Magnesium has been shown to be good for dealing with severe menstrual cramps, so start prepping yourself by taking some magnesium supplements the week before your period. Once cramping has begun, the most effective pain pills contain ibuprofen (in the US, Advil or Motrin), which suppresses the prostaglandins; or acetaminophen (in the US, paracetamol like Tylenol).

One of my best tips is to start taking a pain reliever as soon as you feel the pain creeping up on you, instead of waiting until the pain is in full bloom; this will make it easier to control. If you feel that the pills aren't working, you can combine the recommended dose of ibuprofen with the recommended dose of acetaminophen, since they work in symbiosis to act as a pain reliever. However, increasing the recommended dose of either type of pills can be DANGEROUS! You should NEVER DO THIS, even if you think that one or two additional pills won't make much of a difference! Believe you me, it CAN.

EXERCISE

Have you heard that working out actually helps ease pain from exercise? I know it sounds contradictory and I don't know if it is true, because when my muscles hurt after working out I prefer to lie on the sofa with a hand shoved inside a bag of chips, rather than subjecting myself to further physical agony. But training is supposed to work great for alleviating period pain. Other muscles are put into action when you walk, run, or train in some other way, which lets the uterus relax, which in turn blunts the pain. Furthermore, exercise releases endorphins—the neurotransmitter that makes you feel awesome—through your body. If, unlike me, you're not prone to feeling even more nauseated when exercising during cramps, it might be something to try.

WARMTH

Like exercise, warmth can help with menstrual pains. Place a heated pillow or hot water bottle below your navel (or in the lumbar area, if you get back pain); the radiant heat can calm your uterus down in the middle of the war it's waging in your body. I tried this once, but had the same result as with exercise; the warmth produced an uncomfortable feeling, which turned into nausea, and ended with me spending time lying and retching, head over the toilet bowl. Simply lying in bed under the comforter, dressed in sweatpants and those fluffy socks you find in the deep recesses of your closet, with a book, a film, or a friend can also alleviate the discomfort. Brew a silly amount of coffee, tea, or hot chocolate, hug someone you like, kiss your partner, or snuggle with your pet. It may not make you feel a whole lot better physically or mentally, but it sure is comfy.

4

MUSIC

When the pain takes over your entire focus, it's a challenge to concentrate on anything besides the sensation that your abdomen is trying to wrench itself out of joint. It's exactly like right before you're going to throw up: you're sitting there, absolutely overwhelmed by nausea, and the only thing in your mind is that sooooon you'll have to get to the bathroom to—well, you know what I mean. I was once on a five-hour train trip from Malmö in the south of Sweden to Stockholm, feeling like that. It was gruesome. I tried to sleep, but realized that as soon as I closed my eyes the nausea welled up even more, so I just sat there staring into space, trying to think of anything that wouldn't remind me of vomiting—like how clever I was for not quitting breathing, and how crisp the air tasted. After about three hours in this state I couldn't stand it anymore, so I took out my cell phone and tuned into some music. It turned out to be the best relief ever. All of a sudden, here was something I could focus on, without actually having to force myself to concentrate.

To avoid being totally overwhelmed by pain, you'll need something different to concentrate on. Create your own period playlist! Combine hardcore, angry, metal rock (which you can keep on in the background while you thrash out your pain on your pillow) with dreamy singer-songwriter style guitar chords that will massage your ears and soul, interspersed with the essential period song, "Sunday, Bloody Sunday."

5

HANG IN THERE

This is the most boring tip of all, so I've put it last on the list. But what the hell: hang in there! You know it will happen every month. You know it sucks. But you also know that you're a freaking SUPERWOMAN who goes through the same misery twelve times a year, and you deserve a monthly gold medal for this superwomanly feat. Follow the advice above, do things you like, and don't forget that you reign supreme over your uterus; you'll soon find the pain has passed without you even noticing.

ENDOMETRIOSIS

Okay everybody, let's make the tea and collect the fleece blankets; now come closer because we're going to talk about something tougher.

The medical term for the uterus's inner mucous membrane is the endometrium, and this is a part of the flow we get rid of while menstruating each month. However, some people end up with menstrual flow that exits in reverse: it goes out through the fallopian tubes, and the mucous membrane ends up outside the uterus, in the pelvic area, where it becomes affixed. This, my friends, is endometriosis. The problem is that uterine mucous membranes create menstrual flow wherever they happen to be, and they may even faint or vomit. There is no cure for endometriosis and no one knows why it happens, other than that it's very likely to be a hereditary condition. Some uterus-carriers don't even get a correct diagnosis without first having to see several physicians, because many doctors aren't actually that familiar with the problem.

I'm totally convinced that if men (or at least people with a dick) menstruated, this would be a top priority within the medical research community. Sanitary protection products would be subsidized for everyone younger than eighteen; period education would be a required subject in school; period cramps would be a legitimate excuse for a day's absence from work; and PMS would be considered profound and poetic.

Many physicians aren't actually that familiar with endometriosis. I'm totally convinced that if men (or at least people with a dick) menstruated, this would be a top priority within the medical research community."

---

when the flow cannot leave the body, the body's immune system goes haywire and can't cope with what is happening, and the endometrium becomes inflamed. This is painful—very painful. There are many symptoms of endometriosis and not everyone exhibits every symptom—some in fact may not feel any symptoms at all. However, common signs that you may have endometriosis are: extreme menstrual cramping; pain during ovulation and prior to menstruation itself; heavy bleeding; intense fatigue—in short, your life is totally disrupted by these symptoms.

Endometriosis is more common than both cancer and diabetes. Approximately one out of every ten uterus-carriers has endometriosis, and is so ill with menstrual pain that they can't go to school or to work,

Instead, we know very little about menstruation and all the ailments surrounding it, because it is considered a problem for a minority of people.

For example, there are as many new diagnoses of endometriosis per year as there are new cases of prostate cancer, yet researchers still have not been able to figure out why people get endometriosis, even though this syndrome has existed for eons—for as long as people with vaginas have had periods. Prostate cancer is the most common type of cancer in Sweden, and only people with the opposite sexual organs can get it. And we know, more or less, why prostate cancer develops and how it can be cured. People are aware of prostate cancer. Suck on that thought candy for a while, and then you can join my "Holy hell, I am so pissed" club later.

Furthermore, it takes an average of about eight years—from the moment someone with endometriosis realizes that their menstrual pain is not normal—until they receive a diagnosis. Eight years. And then they have only had their disorder confirmed by a piece of paper. It doesn't make the pain go away.

I once got impetigo on half of my face, and words cannot describe the rage I felt when the nurse at our local clinic refused to get me antibiotics, because she thought it was merely teenage acne. I pointed to my face—at the swollen, pus-filled sores—and asked, calm and collected but with an undercurrent of fury, how the hell this could be acne. She gave me a stone face and sent me home with a useless topical acne cream. Two weeks later the impetigo had become worse, so I got a new appointment and,

already aware of the condition and so get help faster. There is still a lot about endometriosis that is unknown, but if you suffer from it, insist on being examined for it; you might only need a single visit to the doctor. If you experience severe pain, it's better to go directly to a gynecologist instead of a general practitioner or a midwife. The earlier endometriosis is diagnosed, the easier and quicker you'll find appropriate treatment and lessen your risk of becoming infertile. In short, you'll make your life a lot easier. One treatment would be to start taking birth control, which inhibits menstruation. If you don't menstruate, then the endometrium can't get outside the uterus and become infected. The endometrium that is already outside will be prevented from bleeding, also.

Some are lucky and find the right physician, and some people are already aware of the condition and so get help faster. There is still a lot about endometriosis that is unknown, but if you suffer from it, insist on being examined for it."

---

finally, a prescription for medication. I spent two weeks in total frustration over my face looking like Shrek's, and it was horrible. It makes me shudder to imagine having to go eight years suffering from an illness nobody knows anything about, least of all yourself. An illness the local clinic claims is a urinary tract infection, though the medication they prescribe doesn't work, and which therefore brings your life to a halt for several days each month while you deal with the feeling that your body is trying to murder you from within.

It doesn't have to take eight years to get help. Some are lucky and find the right physician, and some people are

DON'T TAKE ANY CRAP

Because endometriosis is still such a mystery disease, many will try to make you believe this, that, and the other thing, while totally dismissing your suffering. These people most likely aren't Satan in the flesh (even though it can feel like it at times), but if they don't take your feelings seriously it shows a fundamental lack of respect on their part, which is something you should not put up with. "Don't take any crap," I say. Quite simply, don't take any shit. You can look at it instead; observe it. Then pick it up with a poop bag, wrap the bag in some pretty gift paper, tie it with a golden, glittery ribbon, and hurl it back in the face of whoever threw it first. A few examples:

**DON'T TAKE
THIS CRAP:**
"You can't be in this much pain all the time. It's all in your mind. It can't be that hard."

THE ANSWER TO THIS CRAP:
"I don't stay home from school on the same week of every month/spend all my money on pain relief meds/cry/throw up/faint for the fun of it. I'm sure it's not my imagination that makes me feel like my body is going to explode. Even if it is all in my mind, I still want it checked out."

DON'T TAKE THIS CRAP:
"You're so young; these things disappear as you get older."

THE ANSWER TO THIS CRAP:
"That might be true, but how long do I have to wait for this to happen? And if this is endometriosis, it won't go away until I hit menopause. I'm not going to wait. I want help now."

DON'T TAKE THIS CRAP:
"It's just period cramps. Sometimes it hurts that much."

THE ANSWER TO THIS CRAP:
"Periods can hurt, but I can't cope and live a normal life like this. Pain relief meds don't seem to work and I don't know what to do with myself. I want it checked out."

DON'T TAKE THIS CRAP:
"You're a woman; you're supposed to be able to bear the pain. Just wait until you're going into labor."

THE ANSWER TO THIS CRAP:
"And you're a sexist asshole who needs to stop belittling how I feel, and start taking me seriously right now. I don't give a solitary shit about how much pain I should be able to tolerate or not. I want help coping with it."

PMS

If you conducted a survey in all senior high schools in Sweden on the most frequently used expressions, chances are "Have you got your period, or what?" would top the list. Add a pubescent, hormonal teenage voice to the mix, and I'd be able to recall the stench of old, used textbooks and grungy toilet stalls. While I didn't learn much about menstruation in school, I knew periods equaled mood swings—that was the most self-evident of all truths, and it went unquestioned. As a fifteen-year-old you don't know much about the wide world around you. (Apologies to all those fifteen and younger who are reading this. I know you're not total blockheads, but you're going to get even smarter with age, believe me.)

However, any fifteen-year-old can put one and one together: Girls + menstrual period = true. Mood swings + menstrual period = true. Therefore: girls + mood swings = menstrual period. It's not rocket science, we figured. This means that girls can't be angry, upset, sad, or irritated with someone or something without having their period, according to anyone possessing basic (or less) knowledge about what menstruation actually is. There is no source for any of this, but for high school students, the words "source" and "reference" are still totally foreign.

The amusing thing is that it is completely wrong. It's false. It's a trap! Everyone in your grade, dear fifteen-year-old reader, has lied to you. Apart from the fact that you might be a bit tired and grumpy since you're walking around with a sore belly, the situation is almost the exact opposite. If there is one time in the month when your hormones are at their best, it's during your menstrual period. Let me explain why.

Every uterus-carrier finds themself in a continuous menstrual loop. The body is continually preparing itself for pregnancy, even if it doesn't show. In other words, the uterus-carrying body is the worst sexist ever. Its entire aim and purpose is to produce babies. Soon it will probably tell us to go in to the

kitchen and fix a sandwich, too. "You can make your own stupid sandwich," is my reply. And then I respond, "My pleasure." Sandwiches are delicious.

The menstrual cycle varies from person to person, but it typically lasts about twenty-eight days from the first day you start bleeding. That day counts as day one. At this point hormone levels are

can influence stress levels and mood). The menstrual period usually lasts between three and seven days, and on day fourteen of your cycle it's ovulation time. One week before ovulation, estrogen levels begin to rise and kickstart the uterus into action so the uterine membrane (where the egg is supposed to land and grow if it is fertilized) has time

---

Each uterus-carrier finds themself in a continuous menstrual loop. The body is continually preparing itself for pregnancy, even if it doesn't show."

---

crazy low and even, because this is a sign that a baby has not been made, so the uterine mucous membrane is discarded as menstrual flow. The hormones I'm referring to include estrogen (which, among other things, makes us develop breasts, wide hips, and that uterine mucous membrane that we get rid of once a month), and progesterone (which acts a bit like estrogen, but also prepares the body for pregnancy, and

to form. On day fourteen, the same day the egg is released, progesterone levels start to rise. That happens fast as all get-out, because you know, in ten days the egg arrives, and if the uterus isn't ready for a potentially fertilized egg then the pregnancy's a lost cause. The body knows if the egg is fertilized around day twenty-five, and if there is no baby, the progesterone and estrogen levels sink as fast as they rose to return to levels that tell the body it's time for menstruation. It's at this time, on this hormonal rollercoaster, that PMS emerges. Everyone is sensitive, to a certain degree, to hormonal changes in the body, and those who are more sensitive will experience PMS, while others might not feel anything at all.

PMS can manifest itself in different ways. Your body might be sore and your breasts tender; you might feel bloated and tired, or sad, angry, and irritated for the tiniest of reasons. I started to feel the effects of PMS when I was eighteen. Once, while walking alone to the bus stop to go to school after the world's

offered me some pick 'n' mix candy. There too I started crying, because the piece of chocolate I selected was the most delicious thing I've ever put in my mouth. This is a thrilling way to react to our body's hormonal changes.

For sure, PMS is not always something you can laugh about in hindsight, even though my life's proudest moment was when I told my "Party Rock Anthem" story to my YouTube idol Grace Helbig and she laughed. It can be hard to recognize that it's just PMS rattling around in your brain. A few years after beginning to have PMS, I even started having anxiety

> *PMS can manifest itself in different ways. Your body might be sore and your breasts tender; you might feel bloated and tired, or sad, angry, and irritated for the tiniest of reasons.*"

most hectic morning, I put my entire music collection on shuffle to have something else to think about; the first tune that came on was "Party Rock Anthem" by LMFAO (also known as CRAZY FREAKING GOOD TUNE. When Wikipedia publishes a seven-part article about one single song, you know it has to be a crazy freaking good tune). I walked along in the February cold, sneakers on my feet even though it was snowing and absolutely freezing, and felt the tears well up in my eyes in time to the electronic house-beat buildup. At the top, something broke in me. I stood there bawling my eyes out because the song was so good. Thanks for that one, PMS. Another time, after a super difficult math test, a classmate

attacks on days prior to menstruation. I walked around for three to four days thinking I was the worst person in the whole world. I was such a failure at everything I tried that I thought people were talking behind my back; it wasn't unusual for me to cry myself to sleep because I felt so ugly, bad, and useless. Nice—not. And do you know what the kicker is? If you ask about one hundred uterus-carriers if they've experienced any form of PMS, seventy-five of them will answer yes. 75 percent! Who have PMS! 75 percent who even feel worse than Tish Simmonds when her mother tells her to "get out of me car," who get hungry or tired or just generally TOL (tired of life). Seventy-five percent is quite a significant number of people.

4

GOOD THINGS TO EAT
OR DRINK WHEN
WHEN YOU HAVE
PMS

ORANGE JUICE

Setting aside the fact that alcohol doesn't affect hormones, the same thing sort of happens to the brain while you're PMS-ing as when you're hungover: serotonin levels take a dive, and most things feel about as enjoyable as explosive diarrhea. Drink one or ten glasses of freshly squeezed orange juice for an extra kick of vitamin C, and you'll feel healthier, happier, and perhaps even less of your PMS. I have no idea if this works, really, but if nothing else OJ is my favorite drink so I'm going to drink it anyway.

WALNUTS

Or almonds, or sunflower seeds. These nuts and seeds are packed with magnesium, so they're pretty awesome—görbra*—at reducing menstrual cramps and PMS if you eat them a few times a week.

FISH

Omega-3 wasn't just the trendiest thing you could eat in 2010, it also happens to be awesome for your mood if you tend to get irritable and/or sad when you suffer from PMS.

WHEAT GERM

Vitamin B6 sounds like it could play the third health-conscious banana in the Australian children's TV show "Bananas in Pajamas," but it is in fact a vitamin that people who suffer from PMS are often low on. Your body will be happy if you take in vitamin B6 over your entire menstrual cycle, and you'll find it in wheat germ, for example.

*Gothenburg-speak for freaking good. Duh.

FIVE THINGS THAT CAN ALLEVIATE PMS A LITTLE

KEEP A JOURNAL

This is the ultimate test to see if you're suffering from PMS. Buy a notebook that suits your needs (a fat Moleskine one in an elegant color if you enjoy writing, or a plain legal pad from the store if you think it's too much trouble to log into your computer when you have to type in the password) and choose three or four months during which you will write down a few sentences every evening.

I have kept a diary since before I could write. I used to draw ugly cats' heads when I was four years old; then I went on to writing fake letters in my notebooks while pretending to be some incarnation of Strindberg. Lately I've entered into a kind of writer wannabe phase when I pull out the journal. But screw all the pretense, and keep tabs on things exactly as they are: what made you happy; what made you sad; if you were hungry, bloated, tired, sore; how you feel in your head, what's stressing you out; what worries you and makes you anxious; or if everything is hunky-dory. Everyone has their ups and downs, and after a few months you can look back through your entries and see if the steepest downturns occur at about the same time each month. If they do, that's PMS, right there. With a diary it is so easy to track and predict your PMS; that way you can make sure you've stocked the fridge for when future PMS cravings hit.

2

UNDERSTAND YOUR PMS

Read this chapter thirty-nine times in a row, or however many times as you need, to learn exactly why, in fact, PMS happens. Download a good menstruation app such as Clue, Flo, Period Tracker, or Spot On (these last two are two words. Yes I know, it's frustrating) and start following your menstruation, your ovulation, and your PMS. Even if your cycle isn't regular, you'll be able to detect a pattern to when PMS comes around. If you don't have a smartphone, jot down reminders in your calendar.

Personally, what I find most tedious about my PMS is that I'm never entirely sure whether I'm being played by my hormones, or if it's really true that everyone around me hates my guts. Keeping in mind how strange in the brain you can become during this hormone fest, it's no wonder I can't tell the two possibilities apart.

However, if you're pretty certain of where and when your PMS will come around, it's much easier to understand why you're suddenly overwhelmed by certain feelings. It's easier to get a grip on them, perhaps because you're aware that they're biological in nature. You might be anxious about almost everything in your life, but with the right follow-up, at least you won't be fretting over the anxiety itself.

LET PEOPLE KNOW

Telling people that you suffer from PMS
might seem like committing social suicide.
The question "Have you got your period?" becomes
unavoidable when everyone suddenly knows the answer is yes. But
if you had a raging fever you would have to tell someone, since you
wouldn't be able to go to work or school in that condition—same as
if you were sick and throwing up. In most cases you can still go to
school or work with PMS, but if you have trouble concentrating or
feel a general sense of dejection, it is indeed a good idea to let people
know why you're not your usual self. I suggest telling a parent, a
close friend, or maybe even a teacher you trust (or who might have
scheduled a test while you're going through PMS). Not everybody
needs to know, but if some in your close circle are aware of it, they
can help and give you the support you need; whether by coming to
your defense or plying you with candy. If you start sharing, you will
not only help yourself, but you'll be doing the whole community a
favor by breaking down the embarrassment surrounding PMS, and
insisting that others respect a serious situation.
Perhaps the people in your environment need a bit more patience with you
when you have PMS, but they can only do this if they know what's up.

CHILLAX

That means to not do a single thing. To hang loose. Chill out.
Relax. Take it easy. My personal tactic is to work out normally when
I don't have my period, and then to boycott everything exercise and health-
related as soon as PMS rears up, until the last menstrual drop has hit day
seven's sanitary pad. I like to work out, but when my body feels as bloated as
after I've hit a Christmas smorgasbord, and almost anything can make me
anxious, my priority shifts to taking things at my own speed, and not even
thinking about lacing up my sneakers to run laps.
I'm stressed out enough as it is and am well aware—even before the
door hits me on the way out—that my run will be neither fast nor
good. So I can do without the extra performance anxiety. And if you're
bothered by the nagging feeling that you should be working out even
though you don't feel up to it, save the workout for the week of your
period, and make it a hardcore week. I understand I'm in the minority
because exercising doesn't seem to help my period cramps at all.

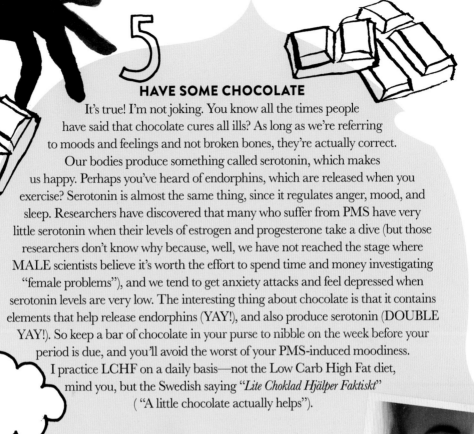

5

HAVE SOME CHOCOLATE

It's true! I'm not joking. You know all the times people have said that chocolate cures all ills? As long as we're referring to moods and feelings and not broken bones, they're actually correct. Our bodies produce something called serotonin, which makes us happy. Perhaps you've heard of endorphins, which are released when you exercise? Serotonin is almost the same thing, since it regulates anger, mood, and sleep. Researchers have discovered that many who suffer from PMS have very little serotonin when their levels of estrogen and progesterone take a dive (but those researchers don't know why because, well, we have not reached the stage where MALE scientists believe it's worth the effort to spend time and money investigating "female problems"), and we tend to get anxiety attacks and feel depressed when serotonin levels are very low. The interesting thing about chocolate is that it contains elements that help release endorphins (YAY!), and also produce serotonin (DOUBLE YAY!). So keep a bar of chocolate in your purse to nibble on the week before your period is due, and you'll avoid the worst of your PMS-induced moodiness. I practice LCHF on a daily basis—not the Low Carb High Fat diet, mind you, but the Swedish saying *"Lite Choklad Hjälper Faktiskt"* ("A little chocolate actually helps").

OWN YOUR PMS

There you have it, my friend—my best advice for dealing with PMS. And next time your sneering, broken-voiced, fifteen-year-old classmate asks you if you're on the rag, you can at least feel the satisfaction of knowing that this guy doesn't have a clue what he's talking about; you could even earn a smarty-pants gold star by explaining that it's not menstruation that causes mood swings, but PMS. That is, unless your period is making you have mood swings due to period pain or an iron deficiency—but that's a different story for a different time. Get the conversation going, by all means, because it's never a bad thing to be a menstruation nerd!

THE HISTORY OF PERIODS

A history lesson you didn't learn in school

'm a well-rounded person. I'm creative, responsible, funny, and look quite a lot like Emma Watson. However, I totally lack self-discipline. I'm way too into social media to concentrate on work for more than half an hour at a time. My willpower is worse than the song "On the Beach"—you know, that house tune by Sonic Palms from years ago? It goes something like this: "On tha beach." And they sing it over and over again. I wrote an entire blog post in 2009 about how bad that song is. So just imagine how bad my persistence is. I checked Twitter four times while I wrote this. That I managed to actually write the entire book that's in

Did you ever hear anyone mention the history of menstruation? Have you even considered that people menstruated a million years ago? I just did. Mind = blown."

your hands should be counted among the world's wonders.

There are so many things I would want to do if I had decent self-discipline, or any at all. I would like to become really fit, improve my entrepreneurship, and, most of all, learn more about history. History was one of my favorite subjects in school, and I was just blown away by how incredibly long the world has existed. We watched documentaries on how the people of the Stone Age hunted and lived in caves; we drew pictures and described the bronze platters on colorful A3 sheets of paper. But if you think back carefully, did you ever hear anyone mention the history of menstruation?

Have you even considered that people menstruated a million years ago? I just did—and I hadn't ever before. Mind = blown. For some reason, menstruation feels like a new phenomenon. I have so many questions. How did they cope, way back in the day? What did they think periods were? And what kind of protection did they use? My gut tells me that Neanderthals did not use products made from superabsorbent cellulose.

The topic of menstruation—just some blood coming out of one of the body's many orifices—has stirred up so many feelings and opinions throughout the ages and cultures.

In Sweden, periods are currently a hot topic. We write books, columns, and op-eds about the need to talk more about menstruation. There are art exhibits featuring menstrual blood. Theater troupes put on plays about period shaming. We wear tampon earrings. We are politically correct, through and through. And early on, we Swedes began to wonder, *Wait—how come I and, like, everyone else I know, think it's embarrassing to let other people know when I bleed?*

On the other hand, the French feel that we're all dopey hippies who have to talk openly about vaginal blood and all that it stands for. At least that's what a French journalist who interviewed me about period activism in Sweden thought. Both surprised and fascinated, she asked why we Swedes have to talk about periods all the time. I told her that we don't. Imagine if we talked ONLY about menstruation ALL THE TIME. How would that look? It would be thrilling, no doubt, but we also have to talk about school, and food, and sweet, fluffy kittens sometimes. Plus, it would be a total drag on days when you yourself aren't menstruating. You could only talk about others who are, and my ego wouldn't be able to take it.

However, I did let the journalist know that menstruation is something of a trend in Sweden at the moment. Indeed, until about a year ago I would never ever have imagined I'd be writing a book about it for young adults, while at the same time worrying that someone else might beat me to the punch.

WAY BACK

A long, long time ago people thought that menstrual blood possessed magical properties. If someone smeared the blood over their body, or maybe over their livestock, it would cure warts, hemorrhoids, epilepsy, headache, and even leprosy. If you were unlucky in love, you could mix menstrual blood in your lover's food or drink, and they'd love you back.

At the same time, menstrual blood was the worst thing a demon could encounter, so if you were under attack by a demon (or whatever the hell happened to people in those days—did demons attack? Were people possessed?), you just smeared some of this magical vaginal blood upon your person, and things would probably work out in your favor.

Some researchers believe that early humans learned to think numerically, and made the link between groups of numbers, by learning certain units of time. These units could have been menstrual cycles, for example. There are some who think that the first moon calendars, i.e. the months, were based on the length of the menstrual cycle. Earlier physicians even believed that the fetus was created in the stomach from clustered bits of coagulated menstrual blood. Lovely.

In olden times sanitary products didn't exist in the forms we know today. Different methods were used all over the world to stop the blood—in Egypt soft papyrus was used as tampons, while in Nordic countries many people put white moss between their legs to absorb the blood. But in many cases the blood

WHEN

was just allowed to run unhindered. Tap water wasn't available like it is today so people had to collect all the water they needed to cook and keep livestock alive. Hygiene took a backseat, so blood ran down freely under skirts and dripped on the ground, or was dried off with clothes.

we, at least in the West, tend to give birth to fewer children. We don't exactly have the same pressing need to pop out children as soon as possible to ensure the perpetuation of the human race.

Period pain has also been around as long as humanity, but in earlier days you couldn't just complain about period

---

Menstrual blood was the worst thing a demon could encounter, so if you were under attack by a demon (or whatever the hell happened to people in those days), you just smeared some of this magical vaginal blood upon your person."

Today, an average uterus-carrier will menstruate four hundred and fifty times over their lifetime, whereas prehistoric women probably menstruated about fifty times over their entire lives. I have to admit, that seems pretty lightweight. These days we have better nutrition and live in generally better conditions, two reasons that we menstruate more often. We also menstruate more because we live longer and spend less time pregnant—as

cramps. That was never an acceptable justification for avoiding doing chores; you'd just have to heat a pot lid, hold it against your stomach for a minute or two, and then carry on with your day.

MENSTRUATION AND THE "UN-CLEAN" WOMAN

Even though menstrual blood was a far more visible and natural part of daily life in earlier times, it still wasn't something that was deemed totally okay. In year 23, (TWENTY-THREE! Jesus was, like, the same age as me. Must have been good times) a big shot named Pliny the Elder, author of *Naturalis Historia*, was born (of course, for obvious reasons he wasn't "The Elder" until a younger Pliny came

menstruating women were forbidden from entering Christian churches. Perhaps you're thinking "good," but in those days church was the place where all the cool kids hung out. The Old Testament states that a menstruating woman is "unclean" for seven days. Everything she sits or lies on becomes unclean, anyone who approaches her will become unclean; everything and everybody who touches something she has sat on, laid upon, or touched will become unclean. Talk about having a dirty community, when you think of how many women menstruate and how difficult it would be to live through

If I had lived during those good ol' super-Christian times, I would have liked to try and stand completely still and only touch things with gloved hands. For everyone else's sake, I mean. It's miserable to be unclean."

along). *Naturalis Historia* is the largest surviving literary work from antiquity, and it is made up of thirty-seven books.

In this remarkable work it's written, among other things, that the "horrific stench" of menstrual blood makes dogs mad, and that even ants refuse to touch corn that has been in contact with period blood. I am seriously curious here as to what type of period Pliny caught a whiff of. True, my own menstrual blood smells a little funky— slightly salty with a tinge of sweat, plus something else I can't really place, but to say that it is a "horrific stench" is, I feel, a bit of an exaggeration.

Be that as it may, later on in history, when Jesus was no longer twenty-three but in fact dead and world famous,

an entire week not being able to touch anything. If I had lived during those good ol' super-Christian times, I would have liked to try and stand completely still and only touch things with gloved hands. For everyone else's sake, I mean. It's miserable to be unclean, especially if you aren't even the one bleeding.

Imagine if these biblical commands were still taken at face value today; how difficult would it be just to go to work? I live in Stockholm, a city of about one million inhabitants. Statistically speaking, about 86,000 members of Stockholm's population of uterus-carriers have their period each day. Can you imagine how many unclean subway seats you would have to stay away from, or unclean door handles, unclean tried-on clothes in the clothing stores, or unclean carts at the grocery store? Not to mention unclean public restrooms, which would be Satan incarnate. How would people even tell whether they're unclean or not? Would they perhaps go through the seven days, completely oblivious to their totally unchanged yet still SUPER UNCLEAN social status?

Christianity is divided into different branches, and the Catholic church has always been a bit stricter than the Protestant church. However, the Protestant church has never had any real taboos against menstruating women, since Martin Luther—the founder of Protestantism—understood that periods were a part of human biology and that it would be unkind to enforce bans on them. Consequently, Protestant churches have never officially distanced themselves from the topic like the Catholic church has, but have still been influenced by the Old Testament in their view that menstruation is unclean. It's a bit like me trying to talk openly about menstruation to prove that it's fine to do so, and yet hiding a tampon up the sleeve of my sweater when going to the restroom to change because I'm still somewhat embarrassed, without really knowing why. During the seventeenth and eighteenth centuries, the Protestant church also claimed that menstruation was completely natural, but still thought it was a bit nasty because the Old Testament said so.

Statistically speaking, about 86,000 members of Stockholm's population of uterus-carriers have their period each day. Can you imagine how many unclean subway seats you would have to stay away from?"

MENSTRUATION AND SCIENCE

In the nineteenth century people began listening more to scientists than to the Bible. Many cultures started to put a lot of emphasis on separating male from female, and menstruation was considered one of the most important differences between the two sexes. A lot of uterus-carriers were banned from education—often they were told that the blood required to make babies would instead overwork the brain during frenzied study, which was unacceptable. It was general knowledge who were of the opinion that menstruation was dirty and dangerous. In the 1920s the Hungarian researcher Bela Schick invented a substance he called a "menotoxin." He believed it came through the skin of menstruating women, killed plant life, and prevented the yeast in bread and beer from doing its job. I'm a master at forgetting to water my flowers, but I never suspected that it might be my period that kills them, rather than insufficient watering. Holy shit, Herr Schick. I will stop menstruating immediately to let the flowers in my apartment bloom unhindered.

Holy shit, Herr Schick. I will stop menstruating immediately to let the flowers in my apartment bloom unhindered."

that a man who had relations with a menstruating woman would contract gonorrhea.

The late nineteenth and early twentieth centuries saw the rise of Sigmund Freud. Today he is world-famous in the field of psychology, but his views on women at the time were utterly new: he put forth that menstruation was "a bloody sign of women's lack of penis"—in other words, he thought that only the dick was correct, and that the vag was deformed and built wrong—proof, according to him, of women's "uncleanliness and inferiority." Nineteenth-century science was pretty high-quality, as you can see.

While ideas on menstruation became a bit more modern during the twentieth century, there were still peabrains

WHAT DO YOU CALL A PAINFUL PERIOD?

A PERIOD DRAMA

MENSTRUATION IN DIFFERENT CULTURES

There are still traces of menstruation's "uncleanliness" in some forms of Christianity, as well as in different religions and cultures today. In some—though not all—practices of Islam, Judaism, and Hinduism, you'll still find that women are forbidden to touch items in their surroundings as well as food during their periods; they are not allowed to have sex; and they are not allowed in the synagogue, the mosque, or the temple.

On the one hand, how great would it be to be left alone when menstruating? No to-do lists, no one ordering you to do things, no annoying younger siblings who want to play fight with you, because otherwise they'd become unclean. On the other hand, all functional societies are built on people working together, and things wouldn't be sustainable if half the people suddenly couldn't turn up for one week each month. However, when girls die from the cold, from hunger, or even from rape, when they are cast far from their families simply because their bodies are showing signs

> *There is an ancient tradition in Nepal called chaupadi, in which menstruating women must remove themselves from their village and wait in a faraway spot until their period is over."*

There is an ancient tradition in Nepal called *chaupadi*, in which menstruating women must remove themselves from their village and wait in a faraway spot until their period is over. Their status is lower than that of animals, and I can't say that animals are treated especially kindly in these distant, poor mountain villages. *Chaupadi* was outlawed in Nepal a few years back, but the tradition is so deep-rooted that girls and women are still being chased away to sleep in small huts until they've stopped bleeding.

If we disregard the part about sitting alone in a hovel for an entire week, I can see both pros and cons in religions and cultures that keep their distance with menstruation.

that they're working like they're meant to, I just feel sad and angry.

In many parts of Africa, menstruation is the main reason girls drop out of school. Many can't afford to buy sanitary pads, so they stay home and thus get further and further behind in their coursework every month. Many girls don't even know what menstruation is, and believe they're sick and are going to die. In India, seven out of ten girls have never heard of menstruation before they get their periods, and in Iran around half of young girls think that menstruation is an illness. I don't blame them, since blood is very seldom a good sign. If I started bleeding suddenly—say, from my mouth—only to be reassured later that it's perfectly normal and that it happens to everyone my age who has a mouth, there would be something wrong with me if I didn't first and foremost believe I was going to die.

In Bangladesh, China, Taiwan, and many other Asian countries, there are huge factories employing thousands of workers, where employees are not allowed to take breaks, even while menstruating, although they work far longer than the typical Swedish eight-hour workday. They must use socks, newspaper, clay, or whatever else is usable as protection against leakage, and this often leads to serious infections. The Mae Enga people of Papua New Guinea believe that if a man touches menstrual blood or a woman who is menstruating, his blood will turn black, his mind will rot, and he will slowly but surely perish. I can't say for sure whether there's some magical difference between Swedish and Papuan menstruators, but through the years a few dudes have had contact with my menstrual blood, and I can guarantee that 100 percent of them are alive and well today. I did see on Facebook that one of them is suffering from a cold, but it's been such a long time since I last saw him that I don't think it has anything to do with my period.

It isn't only in countries far from dear old Sweden that they have superstitions about menstruation. In France and Spain, menstruating uterus-carriers are occasionally denied entrance to wine cellars or beautiful gardens because some believe they can kill the flowers, or turn the wine sour.

Through the years a few dudes have had contact with my menstrual blood, and I can guarantee that 100 percent of them are alive and well today."

So, in many of the world's countries menstruation is still taboo—it is kept totally hush-hush. We Swedes are not alone in finding it embarrassing when a tampon drops out of our purses. We may live in a culture that's open and free-thinking, but we still join the rest of the world in thinking that menstruation is either disgusting, horrible, shameful, or even mystical and holy, which is completely stupid because we overreact to period piffle more dramatically than Kishti Tomita on *Swedish Idol*, who yelled "THIS IS RIDICULOUS!" after a contestant tried to argue that singing well at home should be enough to get her on the show. More dramatically than the King of Sparta, who reacted to the Trojan prince stealing his bride by slaying the Trojan prince, invading his town, and killing off his entire bloodline. I could see myself doing that when I suffer from PMS, so maybe there is a magical link there. Bearing all this in mind, the most thrilling thing about how taboo periods are, at least for me, is that the word "taboo" is believed to have originated from the Polynesian word *tapua*. Tapua is actually the word for both "holy" and "menstruation."

MODERN-DAY SANITARY PROTECTION

At the turn of the twentieth century, city living became increasingly popular and many more towns and cities were built. As more and more people left the countryside and headed to these urban centers, it became impossible to walk around and just let menstrual blood fall where it may, the way people always had before. That's how sanitary protection products arrived on the market; the first tampon was sold in America in 1929. It was not called a tampon, however, but a "sanitary device"—very discreet. Everyone asked, "What is it for? To scrub the sink?" (Joking.) Have you ever seen a tampon—like a Tampax tampon—with its insertion casing? That's the kind of tampon I'm talking about, except not as modern (after all, the tampon is almost ninety years old by now). Back in those early times it was still not okay to touch your nether regions, so this small plastic thingy was made and attached to the tampon to facilitate its insertion. The menstrual cup made its debut at the end of the 1930s, but it didn't exactly take the world by storm because you can't insert it unless you use your fingers, putting them in direct

contact with the forbidden zone. So it was considered a bit dirtier and a bit more disgusting—which is exactly how many people still think today.

In the 1920s, it was common to give to first-time menstruators small parcels containing a few sanitary protection products and some information. Mothers passed them on to their

"vagina" was uttered was released. It was a Disney film called *The Story of Menstruation*, and it was produced as an educational aid; you can look for it on YouTube if you're wondering what it was like to be a kid learning about menstruation in the 1940s. About twenty years later, a few Swedes realized that you could attach an

---

Back in those early times it was still not okay to touch your nether regions, so this small plastic thingy was made and attached to the tampon to facilitate its insertion."

---

daughters, in a gentle way of saying "Now you have started bleeding, but there is nothing to be afraid of. This will happen once a month—over and out." Disposable pads became available in Sweden in the 1940s. They had to be tied to the underwear, which sounds like a great deal of monthly puttering to me. At the same time, probably the first film in history in which the word

adhesive strip to the underside of the pad so it would stick to the panty on its own. Smart! Yay—go Sweden!

PERIOD SHAMING

Why is getting your period so bloody embarrassing?

We're ashamed to menstruate—you can fight me on this if you want to. Uterus-carriers don't like to let others know that they are bleeding, and most dick-owners find it pretty embarrassing too. Even though I talk about menstruation on YouTube in front of hundreds of thousands of viewers, I would still most likely die if I bled through my pants in public. And I don't mean "die" as in "feel a bit embarrassed and laugh self-consciously," but literally die. I would expire. I would pass away. No one would ever call me Menstruation Clara again, as in "that cool girl on YouTube who dares to normalize taboo subjects like menstruation," but more like "OMG, do you remember the one who walked around with a blood stain on her butt for half a day before someone spoke to her about it?" Do you remember the "Poop Man"? The elite runner who ran the Gothenburg Half-Marathon and suddenly suffered an acute bout of diarrhea? (Don't Google this.) That's the type of Menstruation Clara I would end up branded as— namely, not the cute kind. I would have to move, change my job, make new friends, and bow out of YouTube. And then die. On my gravestone it would say, "At least she wasn't pregnant."

When I took up menstruation as my

> *Even though I talk about menstruation on YouTube in front of hundreds of thousands of viewers, I would still most likely die if I bled through my pants in public. On my gravestone it would say, 'At least she wasn't pregnant.'"*

THINGS PEOPLE ARE TYPICALLY NOT MORTIFIED BY:
Having a runny nose
Asking for the restroom
Having a nosebleed
Applying a Band-Aid to a sore

THINGS PEOPLE ARE TYPICALLY MORTIFIED BY:
Having their period
Mentioning that they need to change a sanitary pad
Bleeding through a sanitary pad
Inserting a tampon

cause, I felt like its only champion. A sort of Joan of Arc for uterus-carriers, a patron saint of periods for the ten-to-twenty age set. Not content to make several YouTube videos with menstruation as their main subject, in my offline life I would stride into the restroom holding a tampon, without actually having my period, just to signal to people that I wasn't self-conscious in the least. When I felt the first small, warm drops of my monthly in my underwear—no matter where or when—I would say a small "Oops!" followed by "My period has just started. Where is the closest bathroom?" And if I felt the slightest cramp, I would yowl that my uterus was hurting me.

I have no idea how the thirteen-year-old, newly menstruating Clara would

react had she been able to picture this older, and by all appearances untroubled, version of herself. She probably would be standing there dumbstruck, like when you've seen a horrible accident, with blood everywhere and people crying, and for some reason you find it impossible to look away. Hopefully you've never seen anything like that. I haven't, but I sort of freeze when I don't know how to react to something. If my thirteen-year-old self had heard me talk about menstrual blood in front of many thousands of YouTube followers, a moment of googly-eyedness would have taken place, that's for sure. Newly menstruating Clara did think menstruating was rather inconvenient. First, because it was hot and sweaty in her lady parts, and second, because of having to constantly keep her condition a secret from the world around her. I wouldn't have called it shame or embarrassment back then. Not at all. The feeling was more of being a member of a secret society that performed holy rites in the school bathroom every fourth or sixth hour. Now I look back on my menstruation routines at thirteen and say, "Yep, that was shame." The whole feeling around periods was that of a large, dark cloud of mortification, a subconscious

discomfort that I didn't dwell on. It was just sort of allowed to exist.

TALK, TALK, TALK ABOUT MENSTRUATION

I believe that the older a uterus-carrier is, the less self-conscious they are about their period. Many probably feel like I did at the beginning, which was "the more secrecy the better," but with each passing period, I think the issue becomes less tricky and more . . . ordinary, sort of. Periods become just another thing that happens and needs to be managed in one way or another, even if the person would still rather keep it hidden. For most of us, the transition from "freaking embarrassing" to "meh" is probably quite drawn out. It usually takes a few years before you're used to it, but then suddenly it's just there, a natural part of life. Personally, I was mortified by my period until I was sixteen. I played sports, and once got period cramps from hell. I asked the team if anyone had some painkillers, and one answered, "I have some. Do you have a headache?" I replied, "No, it's my stomach," and she smiled in empathy and said, "Ah. Menstrual pains?"

CLARA'S GUIDE TO END PERIOD SHAMING

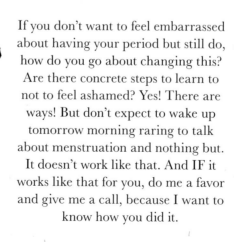

If you don't want to feel embarrassed about having your period but still do, how do you go about changing this? Are there concrete steps to learn to not to feel ashamed? Yes! There are ways! But don't expect to wake up tomorrow morning raring to talk about menstruation and nothing but. It doesn't work like that. And IF it works like that for you, do me a favor and give me a call, because I want to know how you did it.

1

TALK ABOUT IT

You don't have to be proud of your period. You don't have to share with everyone when it arrives, or swap that feeling of "man, that hurts" with mental love songs to your cramps when your uterus begins to riot. It's quite okay not to talk about your period at all in the beginning. If you want to keep it to yourself, do it. When you think you want to start discussing menstruation, you don't have to talk about your own situation. Period talk doesn't always have to be about the blood that runs between your own two legs. I promise that it's fine if you don't feel like blogging about the consistency of your menstrual flow. But discuss things such as endometriosis, PMS, and PMDD (Premenstrual Dysphoric Disorder), menstruation education, and signs and symptoms of health problems to be taken seriously, and dare to speak up about menstruation if you are experiencing problems. It's extremely important that we start talking about this. Extremely important. I'm going to write this again so it sinks in: EXTREMELY IMPORTANT.

2

DON'T HIDE IT

Another way to gradually get over the feeling of "OMG THIS IS SOOO EMBARRASSING!" is to actually embrace menstruation as a natural, everyday thing. Don't hide your sanitary pad in your pocket when you go to the restroom—hold it in your hand like a pen, a piece of paper, or an apple. It will feel like you're showing off to the whole world what you're going to get up to in the restroom, but I promise you that by the tenth time you've walked down the hall with the visible pad in your hand, it will be no more special than going to get an extra glass of milk at the school cafeteria, and you'll feel pleased. Incredibly pleased. And proud. And you'll feel cooler than, like, I don't know—maybe Barack Obama.

3

STAND BY YOUR PRINCIPLES

Once you've begun to carry your sanitary pad out in the open, or started talking about menstruation as easily as others talk about the weather, you have to keep it up. If you talk about periods but still consider them disgusting and horrible, or if you drop a tampon as you reach for your bus card, and then tell your friends how embarrassing that was, you will only be perpetuating the tired, stale notion that menstruation is nasty and repulsive. You have to decide that menstruation is the diametric opposite of everything you've ever heard; in other words, you think menstruation is fun, awesome, thrilling, and SUPER INTERESTING—and live by this.

Even if you find it impossible to brainwash yourself into believing that you enjoy cramps, at least it's a good way to tame the shame.

4

GANG UP

It's never easy to work on making something happen on your own, especially when that "something" involves breaking down and disarming a taboo that has been around for thousands of years. Yeah, good luck fixing that one by yourself. So, recruit some allies! Find friends at school, in your sports teams, or wherever possible; one or ten or a hundred persons who also want to discuss menstruation. And then do it. Talk about it, I mean—first as a group, then with others. Then agree to start heading to the restroom, protection products visibly in hand, when it's time to change. Offer support and rally around each other, and think up smart comebacks to snide comments from people who are not as "menstrually" evolved as you are.

5

DON'T LET THEM GET TO YOU

As to people who are not on the same relaxed plane as
you are in terms of menstruation, it is up to you to be the
better person.

If dick-owners make fun of you because of your period, it's
your right to give as good as you get, but I believe it would
be more rewarding in the long run to invite dick-owners
and other non-menstruating people to join the conversation.

If you—a menstruating person—let their taunts get
to you, they'll just take that as confirmation that periods
are worth mocking.

However, if you answer them calmly and objectively—proof
that you are freaking smart and cool—it will be that much
harder for them to find sensitive areas to poke at.

Answer questions, be a smarty-pants, and watch the
Voldemort Effect (the fear of naming someone or
something) vaporize.

But obviously it's better to consider the issue from different
perspectives, and not just be earnest and factual. Being
able to joke about menstruation is also a big step in the
right direction; not in a disparaging way, of course, but
with a bit of distance, and some empathy too. (It sounds like
I'm reading the back cover of a cheesy, straight-to-DVD
romantic comedy. Well, you know what I'm talking about.)
Look at it from all sides; keep your sense of humor along
with a sense of solemnity and detachment. It is perfectly
okay to be a smart-ass when it comes to periods.

I was in total shock when my teammate mentioned period pains. First of all, how did she know? Second, how dare she ask me that? Third: God no, this is too much, what the hell, etc. For the first time in my life I was stunned silent and just stared ahead, unable to make sense of what had just happened. My mind simply shut down the moment the letters M-E-N-S began to form a word in my teammate's mouth. My nerve tendrils snapped and my brain became a vegetable. I was struck dumb for a second, and then, thank heavens, I came back to life. I mumbled an inaudible agreement, took the pain pills, swallowed them dry and, feeling completely bewildered, I ran back to the track.

lived in Tahult (located about an hour outside town), which is like comparing New York City with the small Swedish village of Mörtfors. To my mind, this was the best explanation for why she was so much more candid than I. Despite our cultural differences, Thought Number Two began to take root in my brain, so back at school the following week I fervently sought out situations where I could ask someone whether they had menstrual pains. As a sort of test, to see how it felt and to observe the reactions to my question. In the end someone in my class requested some pain relief meds, and I asked her, as nonchalantly as I could, if she was having cramps. In reply I got the stink eye and a grossed-

My mind simply shut down the moment the letters M-E-N-S began to form a word in my teammate's mouth. My nerve tendrils snapped and my brain became a vegetable."

A few days passed until I was able put my finger squarely on two realizations this situation brought up. The first one was, "One can talk about periods that way."

It was the very first time ever that I had heard someone asking me if I had cramps, in the same nonjudgmental tone of voice she would have used to ask me if I took milk in my coffee. The other was: "Maybe I should talk about periods like that?"

The girl who had asked was the same age as me, and she had probably had her period as long as I had, and yet she seemed so far ahead of me in her level of maturity about the whole thing, and this worried me. Now, she lived in the city center of Gothenburg, whereas I

out "No." My first impression was, "Ouch. Wow. Goodbye cruel world, I've just committed social suicide." The next feeling (to the tune of a sly "I've got an idea" kind of accordion music, à la French movie *Amélie*) was: "Aha! I've hit the nail on the head." EUREKA!

But of course I had no clue at first what I'd discovered. It was more of an insight, like, "Whoa, this is something I'm not supposed to ask about, even though I'm a member of this secret menstruation society and can totally relate to you having period pains." A couple of years later, in September, 2012, I made a video for my YouTube channel; the title was "Clara tries: menstruation pillow?" and it lasted just a bit over four minutes. I spent exactly one minute and forty-five seconds reviewing the trend of wheat-pillow-held-against-belly-to-stop-period pains. This was the first time I had ever talked about menstruation on YouTube; it took less than twenty-four hours before I was bombarded by more comments than I had ever gotten before, all of them belonging to three broad categories. The first one was "Gross, menstruation"; the second was more like "Oh that, menstruation"; while the third was generally "Clara, a wheat pillow is the best, *y u so stupid?*"

At this point, anyone could be forgiven for thinking "Hmm. I have received a record number of views and comments within the first twenty-four hours, and most of the comments seem to be about the fact that I mentioned menstruation. I should really talk more about this issue."

I thought "Hmm. I have received a record number of views and comments within the first twenty-four hours, and I won't get much money in ad revenue if I don't get a lot of views. I should really talk more about this issue." *Ka-ching!*

And so that's what I did. The thought that it might be possible to live off my YouTube earnings (which was impossible in Sweden in 2012 if your name wasn't PewDiePie) boosted my menstruation self-confidence.

Suddenly, I adopted the attitude of someone who didn't think menstruation was tough; I talked about it for several weeks and received exactly the same kind of feedback in the analytics and comments fields as the first time. People went nuts because I was talking about menstruation—the good, the bad, and the ugly. There were hate comments from people who thought I should shut up and go back to the kitchen if I couldn't make videos without mentioning periods,

while at the same time I was being showered in love letters from young girls who asked me to talk more about the subject.

After only two videos about menstruation, I had my new nickname, "Mens-Clara," on social media. Just the two, out of a total of eighty videos. People began to refer to me as "the one who always talks about menstruation." It seems to be a regular thing—see the French journalist—that if you mention periods out loud, you'll be labeled one who only talks about menstruation. It was the same when I led the web broadcast of the Swedish election for the Eurovision Song Contest— *Melodifestivalen*—in 2014, and had an entire minute to fill with behind-the-scenes vlogging entertainment. I started right off by saying "This is the absolute first time I'm participating in the *Melodifestivalen* . . . Oops! Here comes a little drop of pee in my panties." I thought this was very funny. The biggest program on Swedish television + a young rookie + nervousness = peeing your pants. The expression itself "here comes a little drop of pee in my panties" makes me crack up. Pee is funny. But half a year later, when I Googled my name (and to those of you who say you've never Googled your name, quit lying) I found an entire Flashback thread about how gross I was for only talking about pee and periods. My initial reaction was: What the . . .? I mentioned pee once. As a joke. It was meant to be humorous. Try again, Flashback; I told a really bad joke about a paperclip too, didn't anybody notice that one?

After I did a few videos about menstruation, it became the only thing people associated me with. It's not that I particularly enjoyed menstruation—I

> *Yet without periods, there would be no future human beings. No menstruation means that the body is not healthy. Menstruation is a sign that I'm doing things just right without even trying."*

only started talking about it because I noticed that my videos were creating a buzz; it wasn't something I necessarily wanted to become synonymous with. But suddenly it seemed as though everyone thought I loved having my period, which I don't, not at all.

However, lately I have begun to appreciate the process more. I think it's pretty cool to survive internal bleeding once a month. Sometimes when I have the strongest cramps, I try to put a positive spin on it. Incurable optimist that I am, I try to think happy thoughts between the cramps radiating from my uterus. "Hurrah! My body is working like it should! I am not involuntarily pregnant, AMEN!"

So, I have a lot of contradictory views on menstruation. Periods hurt, they smell, they're sticky, and they make me feel gross. Yet without them, there would be no future human beings. No menstruation means that the body is not healthy. Menstruation is a sign that I'm doing things just right without even trying.

The one time my period didn't come, I was paralyzed by fear. I started Googling "abortion" and cried rivers of tears when I came upon stories about infections and infertility on the Swedish website Familjeliv.se. And then I sobbed again when I ran to the restroom after a familiar, warm drop landed in my underwear. At this point, even the cramps were welcome. They were tough, as always, but still completely

manageable. Like the time I flung the remote control and it hit my little sister in the head, all because she supported the wrong team on *Wild Kids*. My punishment was to spend the remainder of the evening in my room. That was tough, too, but still totally okay. You see what I mean?

Liv Strömquist is a cartoonist and a radio host; she said something really smart, namely that the menstrual cycle is the world's most shameful recurring pattern. She is absolutely right. The phases of the moon: nothing shameful. The motion of the tides: nothing shameful. The changing of the seasons: nothing shameful. (Okay, Sweden's seasons are quite appalling when you think that our winter lasts eight months. But you see what I mean.) The menstrual cycle: GHASTLY. Hide it. Don't talk about it. Pretend it doesn't exist. Mentioning menstruation has always been on par with the wizarding world's fear of uttering Voldemort's name, so let us all start calling menstruation It-Which-Cannot-Be-Named.

MENSTRUATION JOKES AREN'T FUNNY, PERIOD.

MENSTRUATION =

BLOODY EMBARRASSING

Ads for sanitary protection are a good example of where menstruation becomes awkward. It sounds ridiculous, I know, but it's true. Where periods ought to take center stage, everything else takes its place and menstruation just gets a cameo. It doesn't even get a speaking part. Have you ever seen an ad for sanitary products? I have. Follow-up question: have you ever seen menstruation portrayed in an ad for these products?

Me too. Just joking. Really, no. Never, in fact. Not even a fake period. When I think of how often I see bloody war scenes in movies (and I don't even like action movies), I know it can't be THAT difficult to get ahold of a bottle of fake blood to make a twenty-second ad for sanitary protection products. But apparently it is, because all the ads I've ever seen seem to follow the same format.

There are two tropes.

SANITARY PROTECTION TEMPLATE 1

A 3D sanitary pad or tampon spins to the front of the screen; it is zoomed in on so the viewer notices all fantastic microfibers and their fantastic absorption capability, the second-skin fit of the product, and even its incredible scent, so you don't have to deal with the not-so-great odor of menstrual flow. Not that any of those words are ever mentioned; strange euphemisms such as "that time of the month" or "your womanly week" lead the viewer in the right direction. A slim, attractive woman in a lab coat holds up a test tube containing blue liquid, which she then demonstratively pours onto the sanitary product; the blue liquid is absorbed and disappears almost completely while a voiceover tells you that this is the best thing you could ever wear between your legs.

SANITARY PROTECTION TEMPLATE 2

A slim, attractive woman with beautiful hair frolics around in white, airy clothes in a summer meadow, or in a city center, with her BFF. Or she dances uninhibitedly in front of a mirror. Or does splits while traveling on a bus. Or whatever the hell else involves a lot of extreme movements. Alternatively, she sleeps contentedly in the world's largest, whitest bed. But whatever she's up to, she looks pretty pleased with herself, since the moral of the ad is that she can do it all without anybody needing to know that she has her period.

There are several things that irritate me with these tropes. First of all, I don't bleed blue. I have heard that royals are bluebloods, but sadly I don't belong to that crowd, and I doubt that the ad is actually aimed at members of royal families. I doubt even more that royalty actually has blue blood. I don't even know where that legend originated. It must be a whopper. If I ever meet the King, I'll order him to tell me the truth.

Second, it's not that hard to pronounce the word period. It seems like the number of cryptic codes for the days when excess uterine lining flows out through the vagina in the form of mucus and blood deserves a

puppies on a sugar rush because the pads they're selling won't chafe us. After all, the main purpose of sanitary protection products is to ensure that we don't ruin our best pants with bloodstains that won't come out in the wash. These ads claim that we can hide our menstrual flows, that the smell disappears, and that nobody needs to know anything about our period. The ads telegraphs the message that menstruation should be invisible—with the product depicted in the ad, YOU CAN travel, dance, live life to the fullest, and so on. As opposed to what? Lying in bed at home, alone and sick, paralyzed by the feeling of blood between one's legs? Well, something

> *Advertising never comes straight out and says that menstruation is taboo, but it plays a lot on the feeling of shame we feel about menstruation."*

nod from *The Guinness Book of World Records*. But check this out: menstruation, menstruation, menstruation. Menstrual blood, menstrual pain, menstrual flow, sanitary pad. I know it's difficult, dear manufacturers, but you would be so much more believable if you dared say outright what your products are built to do.

And third, as a society, we're far too afraid to let others know that we have our period. Ads tell us that we can do anything we want when we bleed, that we should not let our periods hold us back. This is a great message, so take heed! However, I still feel that the focus of this type of ad is that we shouldn't let anyone know that we're bleeding, and not the fact that we can jump around like

to that effect. Advertising never comes straight out and says that menstruation is taboo, but it plays a lot on the feeling of shame we feel about our periods. Without our protection, the ads hint, you'll be shunned from society. They've subtly created a sense that we're outcasts with an IQ of ten if we don't cover up the fact that we have our period.

PERIOD PROTECTION HIERARCHY

Another thing I've have noticed after eight years of menstruating is that some sanitary products are considered cooler than others. The menstrual cup is "the" thing—if you're twenty years old, that is, environmentally conscious, and hang out with the politically correct crowd; in other words, if you're like me. The environmentally friendly, reusable cup has started trending again—you're considered a freaking hipster if you use it. Without a doubt, you're the coolest

tampons have super high status—if not the highest—especially when compared with the sanitary pad. After years of research (i.e. after years of having my monthlies and observing my environment) I have gleaned that pads are used most often by the younger set, and are later replaced by internal means of protection. Many seem to think that pads are bulky and gross, while tampons are neither seen nor felt, and therefore are considered comfortable and fresh.

Tampons are worn internally, which is why they are the queen bees of sanitary

> *Tampons are worn internally, which is why they are the queen bees of sanitary protection. The less noticeable the better, according to society at large, while we all nod and beam our best fake smiles."*

at school if you use a menstrual cup, because half your schoolmates think it's totally hip (and a bit gross, too), and the other half don't have a clue what it is. It's a bit like when I was younger, the day the richest kid showed up in class with a Game Boy Advance and the rest of us stood around, mouths agape, holding our pathetic Game Boy Colors, painfully aware that we no longer had it going on. With a menstrual cup between your vaginal walls, you're smack in the middle of the decade's sanitary protection zeitgeist.

However, the menstrual cup still inspires some distaste, because the user has to see the blood when freshening up, instead of tossing the product into the nearest trash can. That's why

protection. The less noticeable the better, according to society at large, while we all nod and beam our best fake smiles.

Tampons suppress any odors, so you're hardly aware that you're bleeding; it's so quick and easy to pull a tampon out, throw it away, and insert a new one. No one need ever know that you're menstruating. It's the same with the menstrual cup, only you have to empty it two, maybe three times a day, tops. The rest of the time you can forget about it altogether.

Sanitary pads find themselves on the opposite end of the protection coolness spectrum. Wearing one feels conspicuous; you can feel it when you have one lining your underwear, both as a protective device and when the flow moves from your body to the absorbent cellulose molecules. The moment some blood comes into contact with the pad there's a chemical reaction that takes place that creates an odor, and if someone is very determined, they might be able to detect a smell by your nether regions that they can't quite place. In other words: the pad lets the blood get outside the body. Oy vey—not good.

Am I the only one who finds this hierarchy a bit weird? Isn't it kind of funny how different products with the same purpose can be perceived as providing different levels of "freshness"? It's like if I thought it was disgusting to use cotton balls to remove my makeup, but way less gross to apply the product straight to my face. Or if I believed it would be "cleaner" to use rose-scented

hand soap than an unscented soap. By now you're probably thinking, *Hang on Clara, you've lost me.* Really, why do we think like this? Why is it less clean to use a pad and more hygienic to use a tampon? What if I don't want to use a tampon, or if I can't use one? Am I doomed to a life of un-freshness? And if I want to use reusable cloth pads, will I be even more sullied, because I have to remain bloody a little while longer than if I could simply throw the pad out in the nearest trash bin? The deal with sanitary products is that they are so much more than just a means of protection. Sanitary products are big business—and this business, like all others, likes to make money. We could ignore protection altogether and just let the blood drip, but that wouldn't work

---

By now you're probably thinking: Hang on Clara, you've lost me there. *Really, why do we think like this? Why is it less clean to use a pad and more hygienic to use a tampon?"*

in the long run since we would have to spend so much time cleaning up after ourselves. We could also just bleed through and let it pass with a sigh, like we do when we spill coffee on our shirt, and add "throw jeans in the laundry basket" to our mental to-do list without giving it another thought.

Ads for sanitary products claim that their wares make it easy to hide our periods, which implies that menstruation is something to be kept concealed. But look at other bodily fluids. I see about a hundred more or less naked female bodies every day

whiff of the large advertising posters featuring female bodies that I see every day around town, I'm sure they would smell ten times better than me, even on my best-smelling days.

Sweat does not exist in the ideal woman's life, according to ads. Neither do snot, tears, urine, breast milk, or any form of visible, leaking bodily fluid—which is exactly what menstruation is. The human body leaks, but the leakage must not show—that would be too hard for other humans to handle. Men are not permitted to cry and women are not allowed to bleed, if we follow the rules.

Ads for sanitary products claim that their wares make it easy to hide our periods, which implies that menstruation is something to be kept concealed."

---

in different situations—in ads for underwear, in ads for totally unrelated products, in movies, in TV shows, and so on, endlessly—but there's no body fluid of any kind, anywhere. This is interesting to me, because I'm a totally normal girl and I sweat, like, constantly. My armpits are usually a bit damp and my forehead shines as brightly as the sun. At best, the odor I give off is a combination of skin, my favorite perfume, and the rinsing agent of freshly laundered clothes; at worst the smell is probably a lot of ineradicable perspiration. (I'm looking at you, sweatshirt from the 2009 Midnight Run.) But the bodies I see are always scrubbed clean, as if they're showered three times a day. If I could catch a

This vicious circle loops in on itself. That's why we have blue chemical fluid in the sanitary product ads instead of red fluid, and that's why we never hear the word "menstruation" mentioned in those ads, and that's why we are told to hide our periods as best we can. BAM! Nailed it.

5

IN-YOUR-FACE WAYS TO CARRY YOUR SANITARY PROTECTION TO THE RESTROOM

There are three ways to carry your sanitary protection to the restroom:
1. You can hide it, like in your sleeve or in a pocket.
2. You can carry it in your hand, like you carry other things.
3. You can carry it daringly. Why not be a period activist every time you need to change your protection?
Here are my top five daring ways to bring sanitary protection to the restroom:

1

DANCE WITH IT

Hold the tampon by its string and swing it like a rhythmic gymnast's ribbon, or waltz around in a one-two-three step with the pad. It's perfect for those of you who like to move about, and/or for those of you who are in no hurry to get to the bathroom.

2

JUGGLE WITH IT

See how long you can keep the sanitary product in the air by kicking it or kneeing it like a soccer ball. I'm not exactly a soccer fan, but I've been an athlete for six years, so I prefer the athletics-inspired variation "throwing with small menstrual cup."

3

BALANCE IT

Choose a starting point at least eleven yards away from the toilet, and place your protection on your forehead. Try to keep it from falling off your face while you inch your way towards the toilet. Every time you drop the pad, tampon, or cup, you have to take three steps back. This is a good game if there are two of you who need to change at the same time.

USE IT AS A NUNCHAKU

Do you need to change your tampon at school? Are there people in your class who are period idiots, and like to jeer at uterus-carriers because they have their period? Then this is the option for you!

Take the tampon out of its wrapper and firmly grab the end of the string. Start by carefully rotating the tampon with your hand so it makes steady circles, and increase the speed gradually. Once you've reached a good clip you can protect yourself against mockers by killing them (i.e. hitting them on the back of the head) with your spinning tampon-nunchaku.

5

USE BABY TALK

If you really want to stir everyone up, here's a good way.

Keep your sanitary product in your hand, and speak to it as you would to little children or tiny pets. "Okaaay, we're going to the toilet! Are we going to the toilet? Are we gonna go to wipe up blood and say 'Hello, hello little vajayjay'? Hello, hello vajayjay. Hello, hello blood. Oooh, so much blood. You're so clever. Soooo clever."

10

HANDY EXPLANATIONS FOR

PERIOD PANTS

Bleeding through your pants creates problems in oh so many ways. In my perfect world, we would all be able to bleed through whenever and wherever, and it wouldn't be a bigger deal than if we were to spill some coffee on our shirts.

Our world isn't quite like that, and if you think that menstruation is an awkward subject or if you just don't have it in you to let your ignorant colleagues know why you've suddenly turned red between the legs, here are my top ten reasons for unintentionally bloody pants.

I SAT DOWN IN SOME BEETS.

I SAT ON MY DOG. S/HE DIED.

THIS IS MY INTERPRETATION OF A KANDINSKY PAINTING.

I SAT DOWN IN SOME KETCHUP.

THIS IS AN ART PROJECT.

I BOUGHT BOOTS THAT WERE TOO TALL. THEY CHAFED.

MY RED PANTS HAVE THE WORLD'S LARGEST DENIM-COLORED SPOT

PAPERCUT . . . A TOILET PAPER-CUT

I HAVE NO IDEA WHAT IT IS, BUT MY TURN TO USE THE LAUNDRY ROOM ISN'T UNTIL NEXT WEEK.

THIS IS MY HALLOWEEN COSTUME. I'M PRETENDING TO BLEED TO DEATH.

MENSTRUATION SEXISM

Yes, I have my period.
Thanks for asking.

Imagine a world in which uterus-carriers are only allowed to be mad when they're menstruating. You'd be able to look at every classmate, colleague, and/or person in town and know for sure whether they were menstruating or not, simply based on their mood. Is your request for a receipt at the grocery store met with a huffy sigh? Period alert! Did you just walk past a woman who was giving her partner an earfull? The red lamp is lit! Imagine if all uterus-carriers synchronized their menstrual cycles, slowly but surely, until the whole world knew that, for example, on the seventeenth of each month there would be genocide. Nice thought.

sudden the flow magically appears in their underwear and they suffer an acute attack of menstruation, because otherwise why would they have something to say? At least that's the impression I get after talking to some people who often ask this question. While Uncle Scrooge sees dollar signs when he thinks about business, the type of person who asks this question must picture an army of raging women when they come upon the word "menstruation."

As I wrote in the chapter about PMS, the question "Are you on your period, or something?" is totally a

Every time I upload a video on YouTube in which I question, am upset, or am irritated about something, I always end up reading at least ten comments where the authors ask if I have my period."

After several years of having my monthlies, I have also found out that menstruation isn't just considered shameful, it can also be used as a means of abuse. It's one of the most degrading experiences to be asked, with the proverbial sneer, "What, do you have your period or something?" when you're angry, sad, or upset. Well, obviously, that's how it works: when women give voice to strong opinions, they must be menstruating. Almost always, it seems—even when they are angry, upset, or irritated for good reason. Every time a uterus-carrier raises their voice, they're having their period; if they aren't, then all of a

moot point. Uterus-carriers are more likely to be easily irritated when they suffer from PMS, rather than once they've begun their periods. Then again, it's understandable that your mood isn't all that and a bag of chips when cramps are tearing you apart from your lower back all the way to your belly button—so maybe the interested party could reformulate the question to "Are you having cramps?" It's also very interesting to notice how something as natural and healthy as menstruation has become such a frequently wielded weapon to hurt people. Menstruation seems to be considered a good enough reason reason to take a person's opinions, rip them apart, throw them against the

wall, walk up to the fragments, and trample them.

Every time I upload a video on YouTube in which I question, am upset, or am irritated about something, I always end up reading at least ten comments where the authors ask if I have my period. It's funny, because they always end their comments with a question mark, even though they're clearly statements. They assert that I was menstruating while I filmed the video; otherwise, I wouldn't get so angry or upset. My negative feelings and opinions couldn't possibly exist without being triggered by hormones, and as such they're invalid. Simple logic. When I was working on my research on PMS, I got so riled up about the lack of awareness on the issue and other period-related conditions that I blew up on Twitter and wrote three freaking tweets about how suffering from PMS is not being taken seriously. I got many answers, half of which were on my side and just as angry, and the other half asking if

I was on the rag. It is so ironic that I seriously don't even know what to say to that.

I was doing some lazy scrolling on Instagram not all that long ago. A dog, a nice leaf, a breakfast, five female bottoms clad in bikinis next to three twenty-five-year-old guys, a selfie, a coffee cup . . . I scrolled back up and just stared.

First at the dog, which was a pug. SO CUTE. Then I scrolled down three pictures and looked again. At the five bikinied backsides alongside the three fully-clothed men. I didn't stare because I thought the bottoms looked nice (although all five of them were stereotypically well-shaped) but because I had trouble understanding what I had just felt. "But Clara," some of you might say, "it's only a picture. Three good-looking guys and five good-looking bottoms." "But dear anonymous reader," I'd answer, "I cannot process any more gratuitously naked butts where I least expect to see them."

> *Menstruation seems to be considered a good enough reason reason to take a person's opinions, rip them apart, throw them against the wall, walk up to the fragments, and trample them."*

I sat there for a good ten minutes, I'm sure, and tried to convince myself through pure willpower not to say anything—to forget the whole thing and move on. I didn't want to be that exhausting PC lady everybody hates. It was a given from the start that no matter what I wanted to communicate, those gentlemen would already think I was wrong, and they weren't going to change their minds, no matter what I said. But I'm weak, so in the end I wrote a short, terse comment explaining why female backsides next fully dressed guys is unnecessary, degrading, and sexist. Immediately I got a reply from two other brave souls, both of them writing, "Ooh, someone has her period." I don't know if the second gent copied the first one's comment, but it is likely, since there aren't many variations on the theme that someone's opinions are the fruit of blood running down between her legs.

I in turn answered that they should both take a walk with their sexist, overbearing attitudes and quit belittling my opinions—like my thoughts somehow come from the very blood that occasionally runs out of my sex organ, whereupon one of them wrote back that I should "chill out," followed by, "After all, you enjoy your period."

I spent a quarter of an hour trying to figure out how to best answer this highly insightful declaration, but in the end decided against it. Picture me sighing, if you want to. Do it now.

SIGH

Like that.

DO YOU KNOW THE DIFFERENCE BETWEEN MENSTRUATION AND THIS JOKE?

MENSTRUATION ISN'T DRY.

DO YOU HAVE YOUR PERIOD, OR SOMETHING?

Over the years I've come up with about ten different answers to the taunt, "Do you have your period, or something?" When I was younger, I'd often reply with an exasperated, squeaky "No!" to show just how much of a non-period I was having, and that my opinion was sound. Sure, I shouted the same "No!" on occasions when I did have my period, but blushed afterward and realized that maybe I shouldn't reveal anything else, since it would look as though my period were speaking for me. Like invisible blood was seeping from my mouth and turning into words like "shit" and "hell" — blood that was solely to blame for my opinions on things or about people I thought were dim-witted.

Five years on, it suddenly occurred to me to start doing some investigation. I used the six question words I learned in Written Communication 101 in senior high to ask myself *when, where, what, how, why,* and *by whom* menstruation became derogatory. I realized that I didn't have a clue—and that wasn't reason enough to take it as an insult.

So I've started to take the question at face value instead. Silence is the best response, but it's almost as sweet to hear the unintelligible mumblings I get in response to my mentioning "blood" and "in between my legs" in the same sentence without a trace of irony.

1

"ACTUALLY I DO! IT CAME THE DAY BEFORE YESTERDAY. BUT I'M PISSED AT YOU BECAUSE YOU DON'T RESPECT MY WAY OF LOOKING AT THIS, AND I REALLY DON'T APPRECIATE THE WAY YOU TRIVIALIZE MY OPINIONS BY SUGGESTING THAT MY ANGER IS UNCALLED FOR AND JUST A PRODUCT OF MY INTERNAL BLEEDING."

COMEBACK

2

"NO, I DON'T HAVE MY PERIOD. WHAT DOES THAT HAVE TO DO WITH WHAT WE'RE TALKING ABOUT? BUT I PROMISE I'LL LET YOU KNOW AS SOON AS I GET IT, BECAUSE YOU SEEM FASCINATED BY HOW OFTEN I BLEED BETWEEN MY LEGS."

SCHOOL IS THE WORST

Do you know that I suffered the worst type of menstruation-related sexism in senior high? I am Caucasian, middle class, and generally seen as pretty privileged, and yet I have never felt as vulnerable as I did every month in seventh, eighth, and ninth grade, when I had to make my way from my locker to the bathroom with a sanitary pad in my hand. I did it during class to stop people in the hallway from seeing what I was taking out of my bag. While attempting to discreetly slide a pad into my jeans pocket, I would mentally curse the person who had decided that pad packaging should be lime green and neon pink. After a cursory thanks to whichever god made sure mine was furthest away in the row of lockers and thus closest the bathroom, I made like Usain Bolt, dashing the seven feet and locking the door behind me. I changed my pad and threw away the used one. Then, to be on the safe side, I pulled two sheets of paper from the dispenser and placed them casually on top of the trash can, in case someone came in after me and made the connection that it was MY soiled sanitary pad.

This year marks five years since I graduated from high school, and I know all this sounds so exaggerated. Am I? Exaggerating, I mean? Was it really like this? Was the experience really that tough? Yes it was, but hang on—let's take a closer look.

HERE ARE THREE REASONS WHY I FELT IT WAS TOUGH:

1.

Once, a girl from my class retrieved a tampon from her locker. There were people milling about in the hallway, and two guys from her class figured out what she was up to. They proceeded to follow her to the bathroom, singing an impromptu song about periods all the way there. The next day the girl didn't turn up in class.

2.

One time, before I had started menstruating, a guy rushed into the classroom shouting that someone "had had her period" in the bathroom next to the lockers. I'm sure at least ten guys took off for that bathroom, and then came back with disgust in their eyes, and all of them took turns saying stuff like "eww, gross" and "that is so nasty." I'm 99 percent sure that there were no blood stains on the walls or sanitary pads in the sink, and I can't imagine how those guys could have figured out that someone had changed their sanitary protection in that one bathroom. However, the incident scarred my twelve-year-old brain so deeply that from my very first period on, whenever I changed my pad at school I always made sure to cover any of the evidence with paper towels.

3.

Once the testicle-carriers become aware of the phenomenon of menstruation and the question "Do you have your period or something?" started being bandied about more often in the classroom, it actually became more difficult to have your period.

It wasn't enough that I did everything in my power to pretend to be calm and collected when I left to go to the bathroom with the mission of changing my pad; now every non-menstruating person was on to the fact that each restroom break could be related to periods. This was exploited to the max in the endless schooltime war between girls and boys.

I can of course only speak for myself when I say that I was thoroughly brainwashed to believe that menstruation was disgusting—and that I was, by extension, disgusting when I had my period.

BLOOD IS BLOOD?

My class at school was pretty rowdy. People often shed blood during our intense PE sessions. Scraped knees from landing on the hard gym floor, nose-bleeds from a direct hit in dodgeball, or shredded hands from taking a spill on gravel. Body parts gushing rivers of blood. *Yikes,* you're thinking, *that's just like menstruation!* Mind = blown! Yeah, I know. Here I go again, showing off my awesome talent for teaching. Ta-da.

The exciting thing here is that there seems to be a difference between blood and *blood*—a huge difference. For instance, I'm a master at giving myself

Maybe not all of us would bend forward to lick a bloodied knee clean, but by all accounts we're not afraid to get a little blood in our mouths.

Except when it is menstrual blood, of course. Germaine Greer is an Australian scholar, author, and feminist who once said, "If you think you're emancipated, you might consider the idea of tasting your own menstrual blood—if it makes you sick, you've got a long way to go, baby."
Giovanna Plowman lives in the United States. After losing a bet, in January 2013 she uploaded a video to YouTube of herself removing a used tampon—and then sucking on it. She looks a bit

'If you think you're emancipated, you might consider the idea of tasting your own menstrual blood—if it makes you sick, you've got a long way to go, baby.'''

paper cuts. I can grab a piece of paper, or open an envelope, or just sit around with a bill, and say to myself, like a mantra, "Don't cut yourself." And yet I still do it. Every time. My hands look like they've been in a war zone. So what do you typically do every time you slash your fingertip or your knuckle? You put your mouth against the cut and suck the blood—nothing weird about that.

And what do people tell you to do to make a nosebleed stop more quickly? Bend your head back and look skyward. Personally, I find clotting blood running straight down my throat to be one of life's most unpleasant sensations, so I hate following this piece of advice, more because of the physical feeling than because it's blood that I'm swallowing.

nervous and reluctant, but not unsure of herself. The camera is set on the bathroom vanity; Giovanna turns on some music, takes a swig of water, and after a few seconds' pause, sticks the red tampon in her mouth.

For someone who uses YouTube extensively in her profession, I must admit that this was way smart. Way to go, Giovanna.

This video had all the elements of a viral sensation: it was unexpected, it was gross, and it generated lots of "WTFs." The hate-storm was a given. In just twenty-four hours she became infamous, was dubbed "The Tampon Girl," had her face turned into a meme, started getting hate mail, and was cyberbullied the world over. Those who didn't threaten to kill her told her to kill herself. Facebook pages with names like "R.I.P. Giovanna Plowman" popped up, and rumors circulated that she had, in fact, committed suicide. Periods are one of many issues that are tough for society to talk about, but seeing someone taste their own menstrual blood was the straw that broke the camel's back (or the drop of blood that made the tampon leak, if we're sticking to the topic).

According to the internet and some who use it, it's acceptable to hate people for many different reasons. Like if someone is unattractive, disabled,

MENSTRUATION SEXISM = IMMATURITY

One question is still unanswered, however—quivering on everyone's lips like untouched chocolate pudding. Why is it that the guys of my class in senior high, who were often super nice— going so far as to help me wipe up the gym floor when I spurted nosebleed during a particularly violent bout of Capture the Flag—turned into the worst sexists ever when blood came from a vagina? What lay dormant in these innocent fourteen-year-olds (unconsciously, no doubt) that would give rise to three years of monthly chauvinistic mobbing and harassment?

According to the internet and some who use it, it's acceptable to hate people for many different reasons. Like if someone is unattractive, disabled, homosexual, or transgender. In January, 2013, it suddenly became okay to threaten to kill a teenage girl because of her menstrual blood."

homosexual, or transgender. In January, 2013, it suddenly became okay to threaten to kill a teenage girl because of her menstrual blood.

Naturally, I'm not saying that we should all go out and start drinking our periods. Why on Earth would we do that? It's nutritious, sure, but that could be said about excrement as well; menstrual blood and feces are human waste products that are not supposed to be ingested. What I'm trying to do here is to make you think about this—why is it deemed all right to swallow blood from a nosebleed, and repulsive to taste a drop of menstrual blood? Feel free to discuss this in small groups.

Well, first of all, kids are dumb. I came to this realization when I myself was a child, and there's no need to argue this point because we all know it's a fact. No one can be as cruel as kids. They think they know it all, and make fun of those who are honest enough to admit that they don't know what "making out" means. Children assert that certain foods, such as fish, are disgusting, even though fish is really good and they've never tasted it. Small children EAT SNOW, for crying out loud. If any of you reading this happen to be a child, don't despair: you will grow up eventually, at which point you too will also realize that children aren't that smart. It's not that I don't like

> *Who knows, maybe all these fourteen-year-old sexists want is to be included? To be one of the gang? To be excused from class because of 'headache'?"*

children—on the contrary—it's just that most of them can be pretty stupid sometimes. That's why it isn't too hard to figure out why half the class reacts to that blood thing like a bunch of as-shats; they've never gone through that particular experience, and they weren't even allowed to stay in the classroom in fourth grade during the only lesson we had on menstruation. I'm sure I'd be obnoxious, too, if the educational system froze me out simply because I bore testicles. Who knows, maybe all those fourteen-year-old sexists want is to be included? To be part of the gang? To be excused from class because of a "headache" (which we all know is a cover-up for period pains—yet another way of making uterus-carriers feel like shit), and to have sugar cravings for a few days every month?

If I were a testicle-bearer, and I'd been made to understand from a young age that girls are taught something of a classified nature, it's 100 percent certain that I would have done everything in my power to find out what the secrecy was all about. I would have checked the plastic bag for sanitary products every time I went to the bathroom, and you bet I'd have jeeringly asked my female classmates (because I am a child and I am unkind) whether they had their pe-riod so that I, fraught with delight and terror, could get a bit closer to under-standing this strange phenomenon.

These days I consider myself quite smart. Not overly so, and I'm not super well read, but when it comes to men-struation I know my subject inside and out. It's at times like this I regret not always having been this smart. I wish that when I was at school with the menstrually clueless people, I had been as well-informed about periods as I am today. I would have asked my teachers why guys weren't allowed in class when we talked about uterus blood, and I would have dared to stand up for myself and my sexual organ when it was, as well as when it wasn't, that time of the month. I would have said, "I know it's hard, but stop being such dumbasses," every time menstruation was used to belittle someone. And then I would have shared some of the knowledge I'd amassed on the subject. They would have learned everything there is to know—from what the blood actually is, to why my uterus-carrier friends and I occasionally feel down in the dumps at a certain time every month; it wouldn't have to grow into such a huge deal. At least, that's what I tell myself. After that, if someone still acted like a mo-ron—that's what children are masters at, after all—I would have spritzed his face lightly with a spray bottle and ordered him, "Off." A bit like how you train a dog. I'm convinced that there are more similarities between kids and pets than we are willing to admit.

> *I'm sure that if menstruation had been a character in the Harry Potter saga, she would have been one of the good guys. Menstruation isn't really synonymous with what is most evil in the universe."*

MENSTRUATION SEXISM: LIFE HACKS

I believe that if all uterus-carriers dared be more open and relaxed about the subject of periods, we would have a far better attitude about it. It's obvious that all teenagers without a uterus think that one of life's richer amusements is to sneer at menstruation, because they don't have a clue what it is, they're curious as hell, and menstruating girls refuse to talk about it. It's exactly the same as with Voldemort: no one dares say his name; they make up nicknames; everyone denies his existence; yet his power and the fear surrounding him grow ever larger. I'm sure that if menstruation had been a character in the Harry Potter saga, she would have been one of the good guys. Menstruation isn't really synonymous with what is most evil in the universe—certainly not a villain who splits his soul in seven in order to master the most powerful magic— but you see what I'm getting at.

The problem that arises when menstruation becomes a topic that many people—especially young people— won't talk about, is that it becomes truly hard to figure out what behavior is acceptable and what isn't. It's fine if someone doesn't want to discuss their period; others should respect the uterus-carrier's wish for privacy if they don't feel comfortable openly discussing this particular bodily fluid. Honestly, everybody needs

to make friends with their menstruation in their own time. So what is menstruation sexism, really? Is there a clear line for what is acceptable behavior and what isn't? How do you know, when you're confronted in the school hallway about what is happening in your nether regions, that you're dealing with sexism? What constitutes sexism, and what is just plain curiosity?

It's impossible to draw a hard line. I know—it's a pain. I would tell you if knew, I promise. However, in the following simple guide, I will line up some questions and comments I typically get about menstruation, and I'll at least show you what I feel is okay to ask. I've even scribbled down a couple of answers to the comments—depending whether you feel shy about talking about your period, or totally open—to use whenever you like.

CLARA'S LITTLE GUIDE TO DEALING WITH SEXISM

QUESTION

SEXISTOMETER READING:

A simple "Do you have your period?" can mean so many fricking things, depending on the context. However, there is a huge difference between it being an honest question (like someone asking you if you have a stomachache), and when it is wielded as a weapon every time a girl tries to make a point. In my experience, every time this question comes up without anyone having mentioned symptoms of mentstruation— the most likely scenario—the level of sexism is relatively high.

BOLD ANSWER:

A simple, calm "yes" or "no," depending on if you have your period (or PMS) at that very moment. By all means, finish your reply with "Why? How much do you need?" to add an extra cool flourish.

RESERVED ANSWER:

A simple, calm "no." Whether you have your period or not, a negative answer puts an end to the fight before it begins.

131

QUESTION

"OOH, SOMEONE HAS HER PERIOD!"

SEXISTOMETER READING:
This isn't even a question—it's just a cold, manipulative statement that gets trotted out whenever uterus-carriers try to have their opinions taken seriously. It is completely demeaning.

BOLD ANSWER:
Launch into your best smart-aleck spiel about why this "question" is rude as all hell. For example, "Yes/No, I do (not) have my period. Regardless of what's happening between my legs, you can take your chauvinistic, sexist attitude and shove it. Quit dismissing my opinions as something I come up with only when I'm bleeding."

RESERVED ANSWER:
"Someone is losing the argument, I see."

QUESTION

"CAN I SEE WHAT YOU USE FOR SANITARY PROTECTION?"

SEXISTOMETER READING:

I've almost never been asked this question, since it would entail the asker running the risk having to go near an object that will later come into close contact with my bloody *punani*—the very idea of which would make any He-Man break into a cold sweat. When I have been asked this question it has been out of sheer curiosity, and so I've been more than happy to dig a tampon out of my purse and show the person who asked to see it. However, if the question "Do you have your period?" follows, then I feel like I'm just being goaded, and it's perfectly okay to consider the question uncalled for.

BOLD ANSWER:

"I do solemnly swear on my tampons/maxipads/panty liners that they look exactly like everyone else's. Google it." Or, if you happen to have a sanitary product handy, go ahead and show it, but try to test the waters first to gauge whether the person who asked to see it is genuinely curious, or is just looking for a way to make fun of you—that way you can limit the damage.

RESERVED ANSWER:

"No."
"Why not?"
"Because I don't feel comfortable showing it, so grow up, okay?"

QUESTION

"SO DO YOU HAVE A TAMPON IN YOUR PUSSY RIGHT NOW?"

SEXISTOMETER READING:
"Pussy" is an extremely charged word, and even though many attempt to disarm hot-button words by casually including them in their daily speech, I personally feel that it's not okay for anyone else to use slang words when talking specifically about my sex organ. Furthermore, the question takes on a negative tone, no matter which word I emphasize. It turns into an awkward question that feels like just another way to stress out someone who has her period. The sexistometer reading increases.

BOLD ANSWER:
"Yes, I have a tampon in my *punani*, and its main purpose is to absorb the blood that my body is excreting at the moment. I won't hesitate for one second to slap you across the face with it if I have to."

RESERVED ANSWER:
"I honestly don't know many people who have any right whatsoever to know what I have or have not got in my sexual organ."

QUESTION

"QUIT WHINING ABOUT YOUR CRAMPS/PMS—IT CAN'T BE THAT PAINFUL."

SEXISTOMETER READING:
Sexism high alert! No one—and I mean no one—has the right to tell you whether your pain or anxiety is real or not. That is absolutely not okay.

BOLD ANSWER:
"At this moment my uterus is performing the same job that is required for giving birth. If you get the urge to tell me again that what I am feeling is not pain, then mine won't be the only body bleeding around here."

RESERVED ANSWER:
"You're right. I'm just whining for the fun of it!" Or, "I can imagine discussing this with someone who has a uterus. Oh, that's right—you don't have one. See ya."

QUESTION

"MENSTRUATION SEEMS SO FRICKING DISGUSTING!"

SEXISTOMETER READING:
The sexistometer reading is pretty low here. Whether the person started off making fun or your conversation has just landed you here, it's understandable that someone who has never experienced a period might feel that constant, uncontrolled bleeding is kind of gross. You don't have to agree with this person, however.

BOLD ANSWER:
"Pooping is disgusting, too, and yet we both do it. I have to put up with bleeding from my vagina five days every month. Don't make it worse by telling me that something I have no choice over is gross."

RESERVED ANSWER:
"I'm used to it. The drawback is having cramps, and not so much that it's disgusting."

QUESTION

"NO ONE WANTS TO KNOW THAT YOU HAVE YOUR PERIOD!"

SEXISTOMETER READING:
This is a comment that is often made by people who think of menstruation as shameful, and who prefer to keep it hush-hush. While not sexist per se, it's needlessly scornful to say it when the topic of menstruation is—for once—discussed. Or did you create a weird situation by dangling a used sanitary pad under the nose of the person? Wait a minute. When has THAT ever happened?

BOLD ANSWER:
Launch into your worst menstruation-related anecdote in such elaborate detail that the person leaves the room. He doesn't have to hear about periods, and you don't have to see his face. It's a win-win.

RESERVED ANSWER:
"That's easy. Butt out."

"A KICK IN THE BALLS

How often have you been stuck in an argument about which is more painful: giving birth or getting kicked in the balls? How many times have you heard that a kick in the groin generates pain that is hundreds of thousands of billions (or some other randomly huge number) times worse than giving birth? I participated in many of these fiery discussions during my school years,

and I can't even remember how many indignant teenage boys wanted their side to win. So even though giving birth has nothing to do with menstruation—except in its glaring absence—I'll take this opportunity to clear up the debate once and for all.

First of all, I want to stress that there is absolutely no research to prove which of the two events is more painful, since pain is very subjective. Each person has his or her own opinion of what is less, more, and most painful, since everyone has different pain thresholds. So pain is impossible to measure, and furthermore, there is no human being on Earth who has endured both experiences, so there is no one to give us deeper insight into the matter. This debate is, in effect, moot.

Second, the whole pain levels thing is bullshit—it's a myth. I've heard the rumor that humans can cope with up to 45 dels on a pain "scale." According to this scale, giving birth registers at 57 dels and a kick in the balls clocks in at about 9,000 dels, so the logic of

IS WORSE..."

the highest endurable pain threshold being 45 when you could in fact tolerate much more is on fleek—yeah, right. Moreover, it seems like a slight exaggeration—made by a biased dick-bearer no doubt—that a kick in the balls is 158 times more painful than giving birth. Also, "dels" don't exist, go on for several days and nights. A kick in the balls is a contact that is swift and intense, while giving birth means pushing something the size and shape of a watermelon out through a coin-sized slot. A penis doesn't get torn apart from being kicked, either. Do you know how many stitches one might need

First of all, I want to stress that there is absolutely no research to prove which of the two events is more painful, since pain is very subjective. Each person has his or her own opinion on what is painful."

because, as I've mentioned before, pain is impossible to measure.

While so far I've chosen to keep having my period instead of getting pregnant, I am still a human being capable of giving birth, and so I have reserved the right to be subjective on the topic of pain here. The agony from a kick in the balls lasts for a few hours, whereas the pain of giving birth can Down There after birth? No? That's nice. BRB, excuse me while I go and throw up in my mouth a little bit.

It should be obvious that giving birth is far more excruciating than taking a hit in the 'nads. If you dispute this point, then you need a brain transplant. That's right, I will close this chapter with contempt for those who do not agree with me on this. You're welcome.

MENSTRUATION & FEMINISM

Why menstruation is the height of feminism

There are exactly five things in this world that I'm utterly devoted to: menstruation, feminism, cats, potato chips, and nasal spray. Nasal spray because I can't blow my nose (my nostrils are far too narrow or something, because I've never been able to do it—I would be dead if nasal spray didn't exist). Potato chips because they're the most delicious food I know of. Cats because they are fluffy and cute. Feminism because it is so important. And menstruation because it's exciting, and there don't seem to be many others who get fired up about it. So naturally I have to be—

asking them if they intended to check out the Eurovision Song Contest. Yes or no? Answer quickly.

It's totally okay to not want to call yourself a feminist. I didn't want to call myself that either, back when I wasn't so aware of what feminist issues were all about. It would have been a bit like saying, "I'm a Fooer" but only knowing two Foo Fighters tunes. I also fully understand that a guy who works in an office, and who out-earns his female colleagues for doing the same job, may not want to brand himself a feminist. Money is nice, after all. It makes sense that equality is not a top priority here.

> *I think everyone should come out as a feminist. To be a feminist means that you work towards political, social, and economic equality between the sexes, and who could take a stand against that?"*

simple as that. Someone has to take this on, you know.

Occasionally I meet girls who don't want to be labeled feminists. It's a topic we meander towards bit by bit, after having chatted for a while. It's not like I barge in brandishing a kitchen knife, press it against someone's throat, and yell "ARE YOU A FEMINIST? ANSWER ME!" Not at all. That wouldn't be very polite. However, all the daily papers used this tactic when feminism became hot news in 2014. Inquiries were made among B-list celebrities, who were then sorted and categorized according to whether they considered themselves feminists or not. One single question was asked; no background information and/or follow up were provided. Yes or no? Like

So while I believe that people who think like this don't have all their facts straight, at least their motives are understandable.

I think everyone should come out as a feminist. To be a feminist means that you work towards political, social, and economic equality between the sexes, and who could take a stand against that? Seriously, is there anyone out there who'd raise their hand and assert that he doesn't want women to be equal to men? (Oh sure, in some small burrow somewhere. And to you I say, "Shame on you." Get in line, or I will get out the spray bottle.)

Many of you are probably thinking, *Now, hang on a minute. Sweden is a super feminist country. Don't they have lots of women in politics, women who get to be heard, and women who earn boatloads of money?* Yes, we do! In 2013, Sweden was ranked fourth in terms of gender equality, out of all the countries in the world. That is crazy good. We have it really great here. But there are still more CEOs named Johan in Sweden than CEOs who are female, altogether. Women still earn less money than men, an amount equivalent to working without pay after 3:52 p.m. every day. One in every four women will experience domestic violence. And rapist after rapist is let off without a conviction because the victim was drunk, or she wore a short skirt, or her blouse was cut too low, or she was simply in the wrong place at the wrong time.

Anyone who finds these statistics even remotely disturbing should be calling themselves feminists right now. Being a feminist doesn't mean you have to vote for Fi (Feminist Initiative), demand quotas, or stop shaving your legs and armpits. And it doesn't mean that you hate men either, in case you were wondering. Rather, it means you don't have such strict defining lines between what it is to be a "guy" and a "girl"—those terms confine people into such narrow roles that it becomes a bit difficult to move around. Of course, you can vote for Fi, support quotas, and stop shaving if you want. However, the awesome thing about feminism is that its fundamental goal is for everyone to have the freedom to be him- or herself and to live by equal rights and obligations, without discrimination due to their sex. All this sounds quite sensible to me.

Menstruation is a really important topic in feminism. Through the ages, periods have been used to

systematically oppress women, so it's time to take back menstruation. Reclaim it. Own it, instead of letting it lie out there like public property, available for anyone to mock and be grossed out by. After all the years we uterus-carriers have been forbidden to admit what takes place between our legs, we can start talking about it and understanding the issue. We have to make up for all the years we've been made to keep quiet about it.

THE DIFFICULT TEENAGE YEARS

On my parents' birthdays I usually say to them, "Congratulations! You will never get any younger than this!" To this they tend to sigh loudly, and you can see a flicker of sheer panic race across their eyes as it painfully dawns on them how fricking old they are. Personally, I feel exactly the opposite. I'm certainly not old, at least not compared to my mom and

> *It's time to take back menstruation. Reclaim it. Own it, instead of letting it lie out there like public property, available for anyone to mock and be grossed out by."*

dad, but I feel so good about never getting any younger than I currently am. I am proud of many things in life, but nothing beats how proud I am of making it through my teenage years. I am overjoyed that I will never have to go back in time and be a kid again—that I will grow older and wiser instead.

Most teenagers are probably confused to some degree. If you had asked fourteen-year-old Clara if she was confused, she would have answered no—she was extremely sure of who she was, especially during her semi-punkish period when her eyes were rimmed with kohl liner and she wore black-and-white-checked shirts and knee socks. If you ask twenty-year-old Clara if she was confused when younger, the answer is yes. Oh God, yes. Wanting to stand out and be unique, while at the same time feeling like you have to fit in and be like everybody else, is the height of befuddlement. That's how senior high works. You should have your own style, be funny, cool, and unique, but God help you if you don't get your period, lose your virginity, grow breasts, and start using makeup right on schedule with everyone else.

The funny thing is that all this is pretty much impossible. Sure, there are always exceptions to the rule, like that hip kid in class who starts wearing a bra and mascara before anyone else, and so she becomes even cooler because she effortlessly turns into the model of what a "woman" should be. But for me and everyone else who fought valiantly to fit in, it was a bottomless well of anxiety.

IT'S TIME TO TAKE BACK MENSTRUATION. RECLAIM IT. OWN IT.

"FEMININITY" & FEMINISM

HERE IS A LIST OF ALL THE BODY PARTS

THAT HAVE CAUSED ME
SOME LEVEL OF ANXIETY, along
with their reasons, in parentheses:

Breasts (small)
Belly (big)
Butt (stretch marks)
Hips (love handles)
Nails (bitten to the quick)
Hands (dry, red, and blotchy)
Feet (red and blotchy only)
Toes (ugly overall)
Legs (red, blotchy, and hairy)
Hair (thin)
Face (acne)
Nose (crooked)
Teeth (yellow)
Lips (thin)

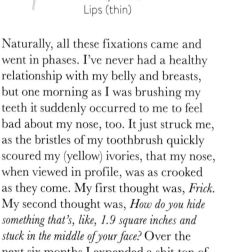

146

Naturally, all these fixations came and went in phases. I've never had a healthy relationship with my belly and breasts, but one morning as I was brushing my teeth it suddenly occurred to me to feel bad about my nose, too. It just struck me, as the bristles of my toothbrush quickly scoured my (yellow) ivories, that my nose, when viewed in profile, was as crooked as they come. My first thought was, *Frick.* My second thought was, *How do you hide something that's, like, 1.9 square inches and stuck in the middle of your face?* Over the next six months I expended a shit-ton of energy keeping people from seeing my profile. I was extremely ambitious in my efforts, and I always knew where people were positioned in relation to where I was so no one would be able to see me from the side. For a project that was basically dead in the water from the get-go, I think I did pretty well.

In seventh and eighth grades, my obsession with my appearance reached its peak, and sometimes I anguished over all the body parts on my hit list at the same time. Looking back, it's a wonder I survived. How do you summon the strength to spend all your time hiding most of your body parts at all costs? How do you live a normal life when, from one moment to the next, you feel that you're the most ghastly thing that was ever allowed to set foot upon this earth?

Back when I was fourteen, I had a very good solution to that dilemma: You fill your top with tissue paper, and when you have to start buying real bras, invest in the most effective push-up styles. Feel free to stuff some tissue paper in those too, while you're at it. Pull in your stomach, and if you've played sports since you were twelve, you will have built up some abdominal muscles under that big flabby belly, so you can squeeze them to make your belly appear a little bit flatter. (As for my butt, there wasn't much I could do about it, but since I was a virgin—a state of affairs I also fretted over—no one was going to see it anyway.) Love handles (which is a ridiculously nice name for what it actually is) on the hips can be camouflaged by banning the tight tank top/tight jeans combo from your wardrobe. Go for long sleeves, that way you can pull your hands up into them so people don't have to see your ugly hands with their bitten nails, and never wear shorts during gym class, to keep your blotchy red legs out of sight. After gym,

if we don't happen to look like that particular "grown woman" then things go awry. There's a very simple way to see whether you fit in or not: you only have to compare how close you are to that idealized version of the "grown woman." The closer you are, the better, and the further away from that model, the more things you'll need to adjust to fit in.

Around this time I realized that I had to start transforming myself. The other shoe dropped around the beginning of senior high, when it suddenly became obvious what I had to do. I noticed that grown women wore makeup, shaved their legs, and dressed stylishly, and so therefore I had do the same as soon as

---

In seventh and eighth grades my obsession with my appearance reached its peak, and sometimes I anguished over all the body parts on my hit list at the same time. Looking back, it's a wonder I survived."

---

sprint in and out of the shower so your classmates (who, by the way, are all drop-dead gorgeous) don't have to set eyes on your wonky body—not to mention your misshapen, weird-looking feet. Again, your nose can never be seen in profile, and when your facial acne can no longer be concealed behind your thin, lopsided bangs, you can always blame it on the cat and his claws. But you know what, when people are fourteen they rarely bother to do any kind of fact checking.

In senior high, a lot of things make you embarrassed. Shame is like teenagers' default setting, a natural reaction to everything that happens around you—whether you can't seem to fit in or you've done something that is just too batshit crazy for a teenager. The archetypal image of the "grown woman" depicts us in one specific way (us being those developing into adult women);

possible in order to become an attractive woman and upstanding citizen. Or something. I started applying mascara in sixth grade and eyeliner in seventh grade; by eighth grade I had purchased my first bottle of foundation, because everyone else's skin was smooth and mine was very, very red and blotchy. I shaved my legs for the first time in seventh grade; I used neither water nor shaving cream, because to be perfectly honest I didn't have a clue how to go about shaving my gams. However, I felt the hugest feeling of sisterhood when, for the first time ever, people smiled at me in recognition when I told them how smooth my legs were.

This was a lie. My legs were in fact covered in red, itchy prickles, since shaving on dry, bare skin is a *terrible* idea. Of course, the others didn't need to know this. Holla at me!

147

TO SHAVE OR N

Young girls who follow me on social media often ask me what I think of people who don't shave. I feel the same about anyone, of any gender, who has never tried shaving as I do about people who don't floss: They're nice people, but they're missing out on a wonderful feeling. In some cases, non-shavers can be slightly irritating, sure. It's the same with people who prefer potatoes over pasta. They can be absolute idiots at regular intervals.

In March 2012, the Eurovision Song Contest was one of the hottest events in Sweden. Not because the singer Loreen won the Swedish competition and because it was a totally epic tune, but because for a couple of seconds, SVT (Swedish Television) showed a jubilant woman in the audience . . . who had HAIR in her ARMPITS. Admittedly, I didn't spend any time trying to find out the identity of this woman, but judging by the reaction on Twitter she suddenly was more hated than Judas as he betrayed Jesus. Two years later, in February 2014, Nour El-Refai lifted her arms for half a second in front of four million people during the first round of eliminations of the Eurovision Song Contest, and again a complete shitstorm hit because a woman bared her unshaved armpits in public. Someone on Twitter wrote "Thanks, but no thanks," that he had had his fill of women's hairy armpits on prime-time television. Others hailed Nour for her courage. Nour herself explained, "It wasn't me who figured this out, it was evolution."

I was thirteen years old when I, along with my classmates, became old

OT TO SHAVE?

enough to suddenly decide that body hair was quite nasty. At least on us girls—once a guy in class had really shiny legs, almost as if he had had them waxed, and we laughed until we cried; the mere thought sent us into hysterics. The very same evening I was back in the shower, cursing about always cutting myself with the stupid

to have to remember whether or not it was okay to raise my hand in class while wearing a tank top, just in case I hadn't shaved my armpits for a while and I had a jungle growing under there. Oops.

One day, however, some time after graduating from high school, I came to realize that body hair is not that gross. I know! Holy moly, shit pommes

I'm writing this in March and I haven't shaved my armpits since November. I haven't shaved my legs for a year and a half. It's quite nice, actually."

razor as I tried to remove my own leg stubble.

But soon I started senior high, and at the same time stopped shaving my legs and armpits so often. It was such a pain to shave, because the hair grew back in only a few days, and luckily I was in a class where I felt secure enough to walk to school on warm spring days with legs full of stubble. Then again, it was tough

frites, and all that—it's a giddy feeling. Of course, there are other people who think it's disgusting, but maybe these people need to take a peek under their own armpits and see if they can spot a hair or two. And if there are some: Oops! You must have forgotten to check under there before you commented on my armpits. And it's fine by me if you want to shave the hair off. If there is none: Good

149

for you! I promise that you can keep your armpits to yourself; furthermore, I promise to not press my armpit hair up against your face. Not only because it's one of my principles, but also because it's crazy hard to do that. I'm quite short so it would be a real feat to reach anyone's face with my armpit, and I try to avoid physical effort as much as I possibly can.

There are a few differences between males and females, one of which is that a male is seen as a man, while a female is seen as a collection of womanly body parts. A woman consists of breasts, thighs, belly, lips, and hair. Hips, nails, and eyes. For each body part

However, about a year ago I took a mental sock in the jaw as I stood in the shower. As I shampooed my hair, I looked down at the floor and realized, completely out of the blue, that I hadn't given the flesh on my belly one single thought in the last ten, naked minutes. I think I know why. I'm writing this in March and haven't shaved my armpits since November. I haven't shaved my legs for a year and a half. It's really quite nice to graze my hands across my legs and feel the quarter-inch long hairs tickling my palms. It's new, too, and a little exciting, because this dark blonde, innocent fuzz is giving the ideals I grew up with a decent kick.

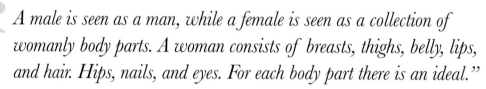

A male is seen as a man, while a female is seen as a collection of womanly body parts. A woman consists of breasts, thighs, belly, lips, and hair. Hips, nails, and eyes. For each body part there is an ideal."

there is an ideal: bellies should be flat, breasts big, thighs smooth, and lips full. Since I realized it was possible to have ideas about one's own body, I've had opinions about mine. My self-confidence has been super low for as long as I can remember. At times I wept and cursed my reflection in the mirror; when I was at my worst, it was painful to do something as simple as take a shower—to get undressed and look at the body I was so miserable about. I'm sure my body never looked weird to other people; I was just one body among many—a trim body even, according to most—but nothing makes you feel as vulnerable as standing naked in front of your own harsh judgment. You're completely alone in your own company, and you hate yourself. You have nowhere to hide.

All of a sudden my brain has just . . . clicked. I finally understand that the presence of hair is not society's idea of normal, but it grows there, after all— and so by extension I also get it that the roll of flesh that suddenly appears below my belly button when I sit down isn't the beauty ideal either, but I live well in a developed country, and extra flesh tends to collect below the waistline. I also realize that my breasts, which look like the ears of a dachshund, are not perfect, but maybe sometime in the future a child will feed from them, and so then it really doesn't matter what their shape is. My blotchy, reddish, pale skin is not flawless either, but that's what I look like without makeup, and that is who I am. All this came out of nowhere; it was obvious that I wanted to fit the mold of ideal beauty,

> *I have grown up in a world which has told me continuously what the ideal woman ought to do, and I have realized that I am pretty brainwashed, but I still can't stop fulfilling the invisible demands.*"

but it didn't occur to me to ask myself why I so desperately wanted to match that standard. I forgot that the body I live in is actually perfectly normal. So while #HairRiot trended on Twitter, I experienced a total body riot. It was so cool. But I also got really ticked off, because I finally saw the influence of unwritten rules and societal pressure on our brains, and how bad they can make us feel about ourselves.

I could have totally rebelled. It would have been really exciting to see how my image would have been affected if only I'd protested against those beauty ideals as fervently as I fought against myself for years, the only outcome being that I looked stereotypically feminine.

If, in addition to quitting shaving my legs, I also stopped applying makeup, fussing with my hair, and buying nice clothes, would I then suddenly feel the world's biggest boost in self-confidence, and suddenly start accepting everything

that society still reminds me is not perfect with my body? Maybe, maybe not—I have no idea, but it doesn't matter because I don't want to stop wearing makeup. Or doing my hair, for that matter. Or buying clothes, either. I have grown up in a world that drills into me nonstop what the ideal woman should do, and I've come to realize that I'm pretty brainwashed, but I still can't stop fulfilling those invisible demands.

What bewilders me the most about feminism is that I have to keep reminding myself that we live in two parallel universes, one of which is composed of ideal images, social structures, and standards. Many of us live up to some of those standards, while others fall short. On the other hand, I realize how narrow these ideals are and how they're used to oppress women, so it's important to be aware of this and to perhaps even have the courage to buck those standards. That's

> *I find that going against the grain is cool. My next step is to dare myself to let my armpit hair grow out. Consider how weird it is, really, that a body part can cause such uproar.*"

why it can be so mind-blowing when you can't choose one side or the other, but have to stay vigilant of both.

Let's apply this to menstruation. When someone asks me if I have my period, I can respond from a feminist point of view by asserting that menstruation isn't embarrassing, and just answer the question honestly. But then I lose the chance to be discreet about something that's considered shameful. We just haven't gotten to the point where menstruation is a non-issue; we still live in a reality where menstruation is constantly used to criticize uterus-carriers. The same thing would occur if I took the opposite approach—answering in a guarded manner because, let's say, I don't appreciate being asked the question—and deny that I have my period because I consider the question insulting. But then my brazen, feminist impulses would have to stay in check; I would in fact be reacting as the going norms expect me to, and the arbiters of social mores would pat me on the head as if I were a good dog. Do you see what I mean?

I find that going against the grain is cool. My next step is to dare myself to let my armpit hair grow out. Consider how weird it is, really, that a body part can cause such uproar. I can't wait for the day when there's nationwide consternation over some man's eyebrows growing too bushy. I will secretly grow hair on all my body parts, and once I'm a famous TV personality, with my own talk show that's shown in more places than the Eurovision Song Contest, with sky-high ratings in all of northern Europe, earning me several prestigious awards (and a pair of used panties from a fan in Trondheim, Norway), I will throw my arms in the air when least expected, and shock the world so completely that everyone will turn into hair-friendly radical feminists. Or something to that effect. But I digress.

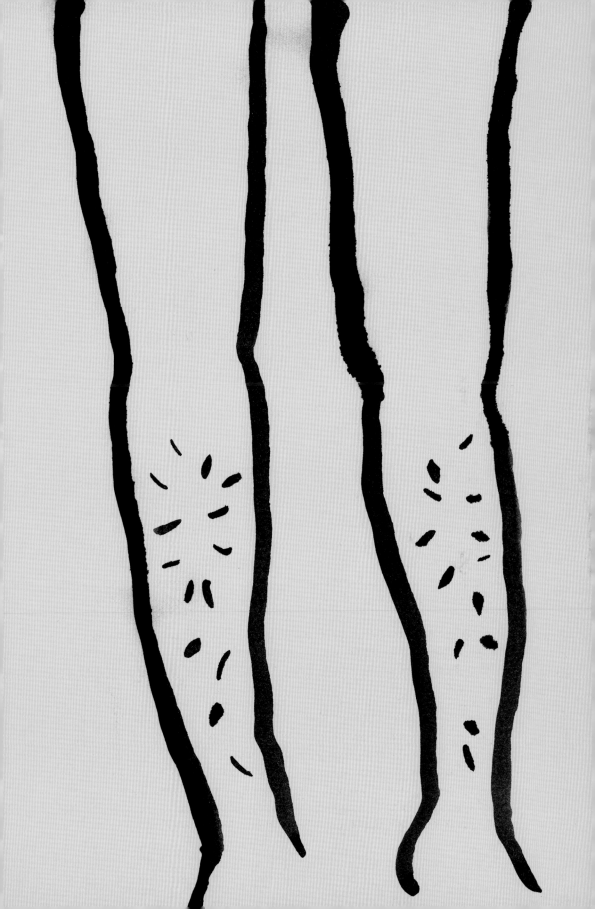

WHOSE BODY IS IT?

I am interviewed from time to time, and I get asked to share my favorite fitness tips way too often. That's the world's most boring question (besides the one about where I see myself in ten years' time, which is IMPOSSIBLE to answer; I LOATHE that question), because I'm not a fitness guru, and I'm only considered fit because I'm slim. I wouldn't want to answer that question even if I did exercise regularly, so I simply say that it's all thanks to my good genes. Journalists typically don't like that answer, so they press on by asking me how often I work out. It's almost impossible to avoid a journalist who wants to know your fitness routine. I once replied that I enjoyed eating potato chips, to which I got the stink eye. Note to self: eating chips is obviously not the correct answer to the question of how to keep fit.

Anyway, do I have to be fit? Do I have to have fitness tips? How do you know that I am fit, for real? What makes you think that I DON'T single-handedly put away fifty-two bags of chips per year? There are so many questions. Okay, cool your boots. Here are a few answers from my own musings, all fresh from Clara's brainpan: No, you don't have to be fit. However, according to society you do have to be thin. Because the worst that can ever happen to you is that you get fat. Fat = a big no-no. Being fat isn't "feminine," either—unless you're pregnant. Then it's okay. Until the baby has popped out; then you have to get slim again—and preferably faster than Lady Gaga changes hairstyles. Good grief, it's unhinged the way we stress out about anything remotely connected to health. Glossy magazines reveal the best exercise tips for firmer thighs; websites rave about nutritionally correct dishes; and there are Instagram pages 100 percent devoted to healthy lifestyles. Of course it's great to be healthy! There's no shame whatsoever in wanting to take care of your body and live well. Good for those who do it, and good for those who indulge in chips one measly evening of the week! However, there are few things I dislike more than stressing out and wasting time over health, because no matter how we twist the issue, for women "healthy" will always be synonymous with "thin."

It's as if it were impossible for overweight people to lead healthy lives. Imprinted behind our skulls is the Western notion that fat people are individuals who eat too much and move

my shape. So it's a win-win for me. As long as my body stays the same I can eat as many chips as I want, because it looks kind of cool to eat junk, especially since by the look of things I still have control over my body. That's the reason an overweight girl could never blog about inhaling an entire bag of chips: it would be cyberspace suicide. The fear of being fat has snowballed so much that it's not considered okay for an overweight girl to be proud of and happy with her body. Uh-uh.

I try to keep this in mind every time I look at my own body and get angry or feel that I'm too fat. I have to remind myself that I'm not considered

I yearn for the day when sentences like 'I'm feeling so fat' are no longer met by 'No, you're super slim, really,' but instead by 'Yes, and look at you—you're so beautiful!'"

too little; they are considered generally unhealthy. In our world, this means failure, at least when you consider how FREAKING important we deem this kind of health to be. Consequently, overweight people are not allowed to be satisfied with their bodies. People can't seem to imagine someone being overweight and yet not wanting to lose weight. They should follow the workout tips for firmer thighs and eat nutritionally correct food, because if one is not thin, one can't be happy. Obviously.

This works out perfectly for me. I'm already considered thin, so I can eat a lot of junk food and people will still believe I'm health-conscious, thanks to

overweight. Besides, the day I do put on weight, why should I look at my belly and feel bad about it? I yearn for the day when sentences such as "I'm feeling so fat" are no longer met by "No, you're totally thin," but instead by "Yes, and look at you—you're so beautiful!"

Some day ten years from now, when my metabolism goes down, I will probably get fat, or at least fatter than I am today, and I hope with all my heart that I will still blog about how "I ate a bag of chips and it tasted so good" without any afterthought other than *Do I want some more, or not?*

MENSTRUATION AND FEMINISM

Okay, we're taking a small interlude here. What's happening? What does all this yapping about beauty ideas and body fixation have to do with our periods? Well, feminism and menstruation talk walk hand in hand along a road edged by menstrual drops of blood, happy menstrual cups cheering on the side, toward a blood-red sunset. That's how I picture it in my imagination, anyway.

Starting your period means that you're growing up. Maybe you want to stay forever young but, sorry to say, there's no going back once that first forty and heave a loud sigh, not quite getting why my twenty-year-old self was so obsessed with a bit of vaginal blood. Part of me hopes this will be the case, because that means that in twenty years' time the topic of menstruation will have become boring; we'll automatically wonder what the big deal was, all those years ago. I will be satisfied with the outcome of my fight about menstruation when it's considered as noncontroversial for uterus-carriers to talk about their periods as for dick-bearers to brag about sex.

Today, my feminist self would like hips—not to mention entire bodies—to be accepted as they are, whether

> *And this self also wants menstruation to be a normal, non-charged, cyclical event that causes no embarrassment or discrimination. My whole body is like a big feminist bulletin board."*

drop of blood hits your underwear. Your body is now ready to give birth.

This is crazy grown-up (even though I wouldn't recommend that anyone give birth at thirteen). But, fertilized egg or not, the onset of puberty signals that the body is slowly starting to change. The uterus-carrier typically gets broader in the hips, grows breasts, starts having periods, and grows hair in places no hair grew before. And it is at this point, dear friends, that feminism enters the picture!

Surely everyone has their own opinion on feminism, and different feminists have different priorities. What I believe to be very important today, I might consider dumb as I get older. I will in all likelihood read this when I'm

they're wide or thin, without incurring any judgment on what is best looking.

This version of myself wants breasts to be breasts, i.e. body parts capable of feeding potential offspring, and it feels like the biggest hypocrisy for Facebook to censor female nipples but not those of men. This self also wants hair to be left alone in places where nature intended it to grow, and if someone wakes up one morning and thinks, Nope, from today on I'm not shaving my armpits anymore, then this person shouldn't need to shave. And this self also wants menstruation to be a normal, non-charged, cyclical event that causes no embarrassment or discrimination. My whole body is like a big feminist bulletin board—I could put up Post-it notes on every body part I want left alone, if only it weren't stupidly painful to pin things to your skin (and then I literally wouldn't be leaving that body part alone, which is contrary to the whole idea).

I started to really think things through when I began to understand feminism. Somehow it became impossible not to question things that had always seemed so obvious. Like, why is it so gross when guys have long fingernails, but stylish when women have them? Why are women's nipples widely thought of as sexy, but not guys' nipples? Why do people put on makeup as part of their everyday look, and why is it mostly women who use it? Those

indeed that is something it has done, at least thus far. High self-five. *Slap.*

It was amazing to finally understand that this is my body—the only one I will ever have, and the best one I will ever get to use. I can do whatever the hell I want with it, because it is MINE. It's a bit how I feel about my room: it is MINE. I'm looking at you, Mom. If I want to cover the floor in clothes, I can. I put them there. That's the way it is. Ugh.

> *I started to really think things through when I began to understand feminism. Somehow it became impossible not to question things that had always seemed so obvious."*

are some of the things I was pondering when I realized that things didn't have to be that way—and so I started to transform myself.

I took things a step at a time. I stopped shaving my legs. I quit obsessing about health. I stopped wearing a bra at all times, because I have smaller breasts and it's nice to let them breathe a little, and it's funny to see how men on public transportation react to my perky, small "dachshund ears." I quit thinking about how my belly makes too many rolls when I sit down. I stopped pretending that my uterus-carrying friends and I don't menstruate. My feminism proclaims that my body is at its best when it works as it was meant to. And

LIFE HACKS

---

*Making the best out of
that time of the month.*

t's tough to have your period—this is general knowledge that almost no one will dispute. Even if you don't think it's particularly tough, there are many others who do, and for each person who has learned to embrace having their period, there are hundreds of others who hate it.

Yes, it's a fact. No, I don't have a source for it.

It doesn't matter how much I write about menstruation and about how great it is—about how we should feel no shame in it, or about how periods are in and of themselves fascinating, sure why I do this, except that it feels good to have a reason to feel sorry for yourself.

"Oh nooo, I'm getting my period next week—just in time for that long, important meeting, and I won't be able to take bathroom breaks. It means so much prep work beforehand, and I need to make sure to change my tampon before the meeting so I don't have to excuse myself, and maybe miss something important. God, what a bother." Or, "Oh man, I'll most likely get my period during the week I'll be in Greece. And there aren't any real

My ultimate goal is to not even give menstruation the slightest thought when it arrives. I want to be able to feel the blood gently massage my vaginal walls, and land softly, like a feather, in my underthings without feeling any kind of discomfort."

because I suspect that I will never truly enjoy this week that repeats itself once a month. I'm, like, a hundred times more self-assured and confident now about my period compared to when I was a menstruation rookie, but that doesn't dispel the feeling that everything— changing protection, dealing with cramps or fear of leakage—is totally hard.

It's tough, tough, tough.

I heave a loud sigh as soon as the week's first drop of blood shows up in my panties. When others share that they have just gotten their period, often in a slightly pitiful voice, I find myself wrinkling my nose and feeling sorry for them. It's almost as if I seek out opportunities to think that menstruation is a pain; I'm not restrooms anywhere in Greece. Man, what a drag."

If you use pads and your period arrives during your beach getaway, then I feel for you. I really do. That sucks. If your vacation is booked and you know that your risk of getting your period is medium to high, I suggest you start testing tampons a few months beforehand, if you feel like it. Buy a pack of mini-tampons and try them out once a week until they start to feel comfortable. I guarantee that your beach vacation will be a lot more fun if you can swim instead of staying on the sand like a block of sweaty cheese.

Back to our little problem. I'm aware that, for my own good, I shouldn't feel that menstruation is a bother, and yet

I still do. That's why I do everything in my power to brainwash myself into not feeling this way. Do you follow? Me neither.

My ultimate goal is to not give my period a second thought when it arrives. I want to be able to feel the blood gently massage my vaginal walls, and land softly, like a feather, in my underthings, spreading out through the cotton's woven fibers and warming my labia like a heated car seat, all without feeling any kind of discomfort. This would be menstruation nirvana—the highest level I could possibly reach.

Meantime, my current, halfway goal is to get to the point at which I can experience menstruation as if I were taking a dump. Imagine, if you will, how good it feels to defecate. It's not nice to need to poop; going to the bathroom to produce Number Two is never the highlight of the day, but the feeling one gets when it is out of one's system is undeniably not bad. That is how I'd like to feel vis-à-vis my period. I'd go so far as to say that it's perfectly okay not to enjoy menstruating, but I'd still like to be able to smile as I toss my used tampon, while thinking, *Thanks, you weren't exactly my bestie, but we still got pretty close; you go your way now and I go mine.* Or something to that effect.

However, we all know that it's one thing to think about doing something, and another to actually get it done. I totally get that it isn't easy to befriend your period just like that. It IS difficult to suppress shame and disgust, feelings that are so deeply rooted in our subconscious that they automatically pop up whether you bravely throw yourself out into the unknown (or, if you prefer, take things baby-step by baby-step).

The main goal of this chapter is to create a menstruation-friendly environment. I will share with you, dear reader, my best life hacks to help you to own your period, so that you'll be able to cope in those shit-I-just-got-my-period-and-I-don't-have-any-sanitation-protection situations, and I will show you exactly what menstruation sexism is and what it isn't. When you're done reading this, what I want your body to feel is "wow," "lol," "omg wtf rofl," as well as "I hope I get my period soon because THIS I gotta try." If you don't experience any of this at the end of the chapter, it doesn't mean I've done a bad job; it means your reading is careless. Read it again. Or get a sense of humor, for Chrissake.

MY BEST LIFE HACKS

The first step to becoming BFFs with your period is to discover the positive things about menstruation and learn to work them. Thinking of periods as sticky, smelly, and painful is pretty simple, but if you continue down that road you'll never learn to relax about it. I consider myself a skilled menstruator; after eight years of recurring bloody underpants, I have developed ten ways to own my period and use it to its full potential—which has without a doubt made me, at least, a happier person. So let me present to you my ten best life hacks, which will make your life as a menstruator so much more enjoyable.

LIFE HACK

THE PUBLIC RESTROOM

You're in town and you
(a) desperately need to pee
(b) need to change your sanitary protection immediately
(c) or for any other reason need a restroom.
Have you already had a cup of coffee or a drink, or had a bit to eat, and forgot to use the restroom at the last place; or do you not want to have to buy something in order to use the public restroom? Then I have two things to say to you:
1. Why are you reading my book when you're walking around in town?
2. This is a life hack: Start by finding a café where a uterus-carrier is manning the checkout. That won't be too difficult. Walk straight up to the counter with a determined step and say:

"Excuse me. My tampon is leaking. Can you please show me where your bathroom is?"

We all recognize that panicky feeling when our sanitary protection is failing, and every fellow menstruator should be 100 percent sympathetic to your plight. I personally wanted to brain the checkout person who insisted that I buy something in order to use the customers-only bathroom as I was staining my undies (or maybe that wasn't it; I might only have wanted to wash my hands, but she wouldn't have known that).
If they aren't as chill talking about periods as you are (or as you're pretending to be), then they'll be so rattled that they won't even think of asking you for a buck, or whatever it costs to use the can.
I've cheated my way into public bathrooms ten times at least by using this very method; it works every time.

LIFE HACK 2

SHOWERING WITHOUT CAUSING A BLOOD BATH

Anyone who has ever used a sanitary pad knows how impossible it is to shower and then get from the shower to fully dressed without spotting the floor, the bath mat, and the towel with blood. I don't know how many towels I've stained after trying to dry off specific body parts before pulling on a pair of underpants—quick as greased lightning—with a fresh pad inside. It seems impossible. Blood ends up everywhere. Ugh.

I believe everyone has developed their own ways of coping with this perennial problem, and so I won't claim that mine are the only ones, or even the best ones, for that matter. I'm just saying they're good. Go on, try:

1. Remove all clothes except your panties.

2. Sit down on the toilet.

3. Throw away your used pad, place a fresh pad in your underwear, and set them within easy reach of the toilet.

4. Pull off a few strips of toilet tissue, and scrunch them together into two balls.

5. Squeeze one ball between your legs, and hold the other ball in your hand.

6 Move from the toilet to the shower.

7. Throw away the ball from between your legs, and let the blood run.

8. Place the other ball as far away as possible from the showerhead, but still near enough so you can reach for it while you still have both your feet inside the shower, preferably next to the towel you're going to use to dry off with.

9. Shower.

10. Reach for ball number two, and hold it while rinsing your lower body free of any streaks of blood.

11. Quick as a flash, squeeze ball number two in between your legs.

12. Move from the shower to the toilet.

13 Clean yourself off on the toilet, and pull on the underwear with the new pad.

Ta-da! No more unintentional blood stains.

Oh yes, before I forget: make sure that you find and throw away the first paper ball—the one you tossed aside before you got into shower. I know from experience that some people, dads for example, don't love stepping on blood-soaked toilet paper.

LIFE HACK

PERIOD TREATS

This is one of the best tricks to make menstruation your
BFF instead of your frenemy. In short, this is about you
starting to see yourself as a dog. Get down on the floor
and make like Fido! Just kidding. But you know how dogs
are rewarded when they do something good? If I say "sit"
and the dog sits, I'll give him a treat. That way the dog
learns that it's good to obey, because when he does he gets
a reward. I have created a tactic that works the same way
to manipulate myself into enjoying menstruation week. I
set things aside specifically for that week. If I've been to the
mall and bought a badass sweater, I might wait until I get
my period to wear it, so at least I can feel sassy while my
uterus is tearing me apart. Or if I have half a bag of chips
left over from the weekend, I might say to myself, "I can
either finish them off now simply because I like them, or I
can wait until my period gets here in four days' time and
have a little party with my belly," which usually means that
I leave the chips alone and feel extra happy four days later.
I'm gradually teaching my body that it is nice to menstruate, because then I get to enjoy things. It's a bit like celebrating your birthday once a month.

In my next life I want to come back as a dog, for realz.

LIFE HACK

4

EXPLOIT YOUR PMS

During the entirety of my fertile life thus far, I have never found anything remotely pleasant about having PMS. I feel down and tired, and I want nothing more than to stay in bed and sleep. PMS days are my worst of the month, not only because I am so TOL (Tired of Life) that I don't have the strength to do anything, but also because all my creativity and sense of humor vaporize. I've attempted to video blog when I have PMS and have decided to quit trying, because it always ends with me in tears while I'm editing because I can't get over how dreadful and boring I am. Every time.

That's why I experienced a true revelation the other day when I spoke to Josefin Persdotter, a scientist whose research focuses primarily on menstruation. One of her pieces of advice is to go to the movies when you have PMS, because the experience will be so much more rewarding than if you're otherwise hormonally balanced. When something sad occurs, you'll sit in your seat and cry your eyes out, and if there's a happy ending for the characters, you too will feel happy, for the rest of the day. The same goes for war games, according to Josefin. Killing a few virtual soldiers is far more satisfying when you have PMS, and helps get rid of all the pent-up aggression. I can proudly say that, for the first time in my life, I'm looking forward to my PMS, simply because I'll have the opportunity to test run this life hack.

LIFE HACK

EXPLOIT YOUR PMS 2.0

I'll continue on the PMS theme. Personally, I always have to get through three or four day of PMS right before my period, and I often know exactly when my period will arrive because I'll wake in the morning and suddenly realize my first feeling of the day is no longer anxiety. In the same way I've learned to link period cramping to rewards (see Life Hack #3), I equate feelings of relief and freedom with "goodbye PMS, hello blood." Out of the clear blue I feel lust for life, and I've taught myself to take advantage of that—to the max. I channel my renewed sense of optimism into my schoolwork, creative endeavors, and work projects.

I always get a crazy amount of things done the day after PMS. You cannot imagine what a big chunk of this book was written on the first day of my period. Sometimes I even kind of enjoy vacuuming, which says a lot.

LIFE HACK 6

PERIOD PANTIES

On numerous occasions I have heard uterus-carriers talk about having specific "period panties." These are the most unlovely undergarments of their wardrobe; they're at the bottom of the pile and would never see the light of day were it not for a few select days of the month. Every time I hear of these period panties I'm not enthused by the idea. I'm not even sure I fully understand it. Like, why do I have to wear ugly drawers just because I have my period? What if I only own pretty, comfortable panties—do I have to go get some ugly, uncomfortable ones to wear during my period? Or, looking at it from another perspective, which makes the whole thing even worse: if pretty panties mean uncomfortable tiny lacy thongs, and ugly panties mean big cotton granny panties, is it then my duty as "woman" to wear uncomfortable underwear three weeks out of every month, and comfortable panties for only one week because it's the only week I'm allowed to "let myself go"? Is it because I'm not "available," or what? No, this really ticks me off. This is why I don't agree with the concept of period panties. Grrr.

On the other hand, I've come to realize that period panties are super useful if, like me, you bleed a ton. I used to own two pairs of brown-and-turquoise patterned panties when my periods began. Well, I owned a lot of underwear, but I often wore these two in particular. The weird thing was that I always managed to bleed through if I wore them when I menstruated. After owning them for about a year, I could open the door to my closet, pick out a pair of panties, realize it was one of the patterned pair of panties, and think, *Okay, then, today I'm probably going to bleed through my sanitary protection.* And I did, every single time. They were weird freaking panties, if you ask me. In the end I wore them as night panties during the first part of my period. I always used to bleed through the first nights, and had to sleep on a towel so I wouldn't stain my mattress. Since these undies already had stains from many previous leakages, it felt okay to wake up in a pool of my own blood without having to worry about ruining my underwear. If you know that you're prone to leaking, save your worn-out panties instead of throwing them away, and start using them as period panties instead. I was mostly glad that I wore my old drawers when blood missed the pad; all those stains gave them a welcome aesthetic change—plus, I could congratulate myself in that my best, most comfortable frillies didn't get stains that were too hard to remove.

LIFE HACK

WANDERLUST-Y OVERNIGHT PADS

The overnight pad is an amazing invention! When I use a tampon, I need to keep an eye on the clock so I know when to go to the bathroom to change before I start leaking. But even for someone (like me!) who bleeds more heavily than Leona Lewis's love, there are pads in bigger sizes that allow me to sleep for eight hours, so that I don't have to set the alarm and run to the john. What is not so good about overnight pads, regardless of their absorption, is that most of them seem to be developed for dead monster fish. Or at least for people who sleep like dead monster fish. I don't sleep like dead monster fish, and I can't count the times I've woken up with blood down to the back of my knees, and found that my pad—still drier than dust—somehow managed to travel up to rest in my lumbar region. "What the hell are you doing there?" I ask the pad. "No idea!" is its answer. "Same here," I say. And then I start to wonder what my body has been up to while I was asleep.

Most people shift around when they sleep. If the pad won't stay in place when you start tossing and turning, pull on another pair of underpants before you hit the sack, so it can keep the first pair of undies, with the pad, in their proper place.

LIFE HACK 8

MINI-TAM[PONS] ARE SUP[ER] EFFICIEN[T] STOPPIN[G] NOSEBLE[EDS]

1PONS RISINGLY T AT G EDS.

LIFE HACKS

171

LIFE HACK

FRESH NETHERS

No matter how often ads for sanitary protection insist that their pads are the freshest—they're not. It is all a big lie. There are no fresh pads. Don't believe it, kids. Things will always be sweaty and cooped up Down There when you have your period, and there's not much you can do about it. Pads might feature a delicate scent of chamomile at a first whiff, but after two hours and a tablespoon of menstrual blood, that sweet perfume will be long gone.

So what to do when the claustrophobia becomes overwhelming? Buy a pack of unscented baby wipes and keep them in your purse. As it happens, baby wipes work perfectly well as adult wipes, too. It's kind of like a day spa for our downstairs. Fresh!

LIFE HACK 10

A HAIR IN YOUR MOUTH

There's nothing weird about being embarrassed about menstruation. It's difficult to let go of all the subliminal messages we absorb along the way. Anyone who claims they've never felt embarrassed about their period is lying. Even if one wants to be completely open about it, it's also okay not to be, or to not talk about it all the time. Opting to follow the norm doesn't, like, make you a bad person. But it is good to be able to talk about it sometimes, especially as you could end up in a sticky situation (as it were) if you don't get your hands on something to protect your panties within the next five minutes. If you find it very awkward to ask for a tampon, or if you have colleagues or classmates who haven't yet learned to treat the topic of menstruation in an adult fashion, then you have all the right in the world to not utter the letters M-E-N-S-T-R-U-A-T-I-O-N. Instead, establish code words for the various things you need—expressions that only you and those closest to you are in on. For example, if you want to say:

"Hi, I think I just got my period. Does anyone have a tampon I can borrow?"

To avoid mortifying situations, or ignorant non-uterus-carriers who should just get lost, this is what you can say with code words:

"Hi, I think I just got a hair in my mouth.
Does anyone have some floss I can borrow?"

Nobody is going to snicker or jeer; no one will even react to you having a hair in your mouth. You have the power when using your own language, see? I promise that if you actively use the following ten tips, you'll be ready to bury the hatchet and make peace with your period faster than you can shout "Cramps!"
Now this isn't a promotional film—I won't see one red penny from all of you here making friends with your period thanks to my Life Hacks, but part of me is totally delighted with this list anyway. I kind of want to sell you on it, even though I don't need to. Before I die, I should try to get a job as a telemarketer. Something tells me that it would be right up my alley.

CLARA'S SIMPLE 10-STEP GUIDE

FOR TIMES WHEN YOU'RE AMBUSHED BY YOUR PERIOD AND YOU DON'T HAVE ANY SANITARY PROTECTION ON HAND

1.
FIND A BATHROOM.
PUT TOILET PAPER IN YOUR UNDERPANTS.

2.
CAN'T FIND A BATHROOM? SQUEEZE TIGHT.
IT WON'T HELP,
BUT IT WILL FEEL LIKE IT DOES.

3.
**ASK A FRIEND OR FAMILY MEMBER
FOR A TAMPON OR A PAD.**

4.
NO FRIEND OR FAMILY MEMBER PRESENT?
ASK SOMEONE ELSE FOR A TAMPON OR A PAD.

5.
DON'T DARE ASK?
TRICKY. SQUEEZE.

6.
DON'T COUGH. DON'T SNEEZE.

7.
LOCATE THE NEAREST GROCERY STORE OR PHARMACY.
RUN THERE—BUT NOT TOO QUICKLY—PREFERABLY WITH YOUR
THIGHS PRESSED TOGETHER SO NO DROP CAN ESCAPE.

8.
**CAN'T RUN TO THE STORE BECAUSE YOU'RE IN A CLASS,
A MEETING, OR WHATEVER?**
THERE IS BOUND TO BE SOMEONE THERE WHO CAN HELP YOU.
GO BACK TO POINT THREE.

9.
**CAN'T RUN TO THE STORE BECAUSE YOU'RE ALONE
IN THE MIDDLE OF THE DESERT, ON THE SAVANNAH,
IN THE MOUNTAINS, OR AT ANOTHER DESERTED SITE?**
PITY. PICK SOME MOSS OR A STONE OR SOMETHING,
AND SECURE IN YOUR UNDERWEAR.

10.
CHOOSE TO NOT DO ANY OF THE ABOVE?
WELL, THEN YOU CAN BLOODY WELL LET IT RUN
BECAUSE I AM ALL OUT SUGGESTIONS.
WHO DO YOU THINK I AM, GOD HIMSELF?

INTERNATIONAL MENSTRUAL

I've given you tons of great tips on how to become buddies with your period. Do you still feel that you're not quite there yet? Do you feel like you're one of two people in a clique who hang out simply because you're a part of the same circle of friends, but never quite get along? Then I have one last tip for you! Circle May 28 on your calendar and get ready for something AMAZING.

The world's first Menstrual Hygiene Day was held May 28, 2014. Sure, it was created to draw attention to the lack of education about sanitary protection in developing countries, and to strengthen the rights of uterus-carriers in handling their periods safely, privately, and with dignity, but that doesn't mean that we in the Western world can't also take part in it. I don't know about you, but I will be celebrating May 28 as if it were a national holiday. Here are five ways you can celebrate that day, too:

DO SOMETHING FOR CHARITY. Donating money, whether through an ambitious collection or by contributing a fiver, is one of the simplest and quickest ways to help people in other parts of the world improve their lot. For example, check out WaterAid's homepage. They work to get everyone access to clean water, which is super important for menstruators in developing countries so they can avoid infections and change sanitary protection at school. Or, if you're tempted to buy a menstrual cup, choose a Ruby Cup to honor the day. For each cup sold, the company will donate a cup to girls in Kenya. This is very smart, in my opinion. There are oodles of different organizations that are helping to improve menstruation conditions; do a Google search to find them.

THROW A MENSTRUATION PARTY. Gather some friends, both menstruators and non-menstruators (so you can teach them some sense) and plan an evening full of period-themed activities. Place the egg in the ovary (like pinning the tail on the donkey, but with different visuals); enjoy some red punch; uterus-carriers can play musical chairs; or teach and learn feminist self-defense moves. The possibilities are endless. Also, don't forget what might be the most important of all: Instagram like

HYGIENE DAY

crazy about all the menstruation-related activities you're involved in, so that those who are not aware of this holiday get jealous and want to join in the shark week celebrations.

TAKE A MENSTRUATION QUIZ.
Any social studies or history teacher won't hesitate to sanction this as legitimate class material. Set up teams and compete by answering questions such as "Why is Menstrual Hygiene Day held on May 28th?" (Answer: Because May is the fifth month of the year, which is the average number of days for a period, and a typical menstrual cycle lasts twenty-eight days). The team that gets most correct answers wins a chocolate bar and some pain relievers.

GET CRAFTY.
Visit a hobby store and purchase some clay, paint, jewelry chains, and earring hooks. Sit yourself down and channel your inner Picasso; bring out your most creative side and assemble your very own gorgeous menstruation-themed jewelry. How about a pair of tampon earrings, or pussy necklace? Yes please! This is fun even if you're not creative or crafty, because even if it comes out looking like garbage, you can always call it abstract art. If there is anything in life that's abstract, it's fricking menstruation.

PAY HOMAGE TO YOUR PERIOD.
Do you have your period during Menstrual Hygiene Day? OMG! Your timing couldn't be better. This is the best way to honor this day. This might totally sound like a piece of grandma's advice, but give the sanitary protection between your legs some extra attention. Send the inventor of this product a loving thought, and give thanks for your lot in life. It's easier to be happy about things when you realize that due to this contraption in your panties you can go to school, hang out with your friends, go to the gym and exercise, or just chill out at home on the couch, without any of it being a big hassle. You will never love your period and your protection more than on May 28. Carpe diem. (Nah, I think that went a bit too far. I take that last statement back.)

5 TIPS

FOR IF YOU HAVE

YOUR PERIOD

AND WANT TO HAVE SEX

1

**BUY A TOWEL
(PREFERABLY A RED ONE)**

Place it on the bed. Tuck it in along the long sides of the bed, like a misshapen sheet. Go nuts.

DO IT IN THE SHOWER

This is a bit more physically strenuous (you have to stand up . . . ugh), but it might feel a bit more daring if you tend to not do it anywhere else than in bed. Be warned, though, that you might be in for a fight over who'll be standing under the showerhead—it should be you, naturally; the one who loses that fight might get a bit chilly.

3
TAKE AN ICE-COLD SHOWER RIGHT BEFORE

I once read that it's good for your hair to finish your shower by rinsing your hair in ice-cold water. I tried it, and oh, the horror. Thank heavens for warm water. However, I had my period while I tried this, and believe it or not, it put a quick stop to my flow. Okay, I know that sounds like a big April Fool's joke, but I have a theory. Will those who have heard that testicles draw up and "disappear" when it's cold, like when a dick-bearer swims outside, raise their hand? This is a fascinating phenomenon, and it seems that it happens because testicles are "the most precious part of the male body" (if we want to be cisnormative) and need to be shield-ed from the cold. My theory is that uterus-carrying bodies function in a similar way. Five minutes after the cold shower, I was bleeding freely again. I have no idea whether the flow stopped because my body just felt like it, or if it can be postu-lated that even vajayjays/vaginal passages/uteruses contract in a cold environment, but it's worth a ponder. If you have the time, excuse yourself, sprint to the bathroom, take an ice-cold shower for about a minute, and then run back—before your partner gets fed up, that is.

4
TIME IT FOR A STAY AT A HOTEL

If you ever stay at a hotel and end up in a sexy situation, go ahead and muck up the sheets as you see fit; they'll be changed the next day anyway, either by a cleaner or by a maid who hopefully doesn't suffer from a blood phobia.

5
PLAY VAMPIRE

This is perfect if you like roleplay. It might even be something worth considering if you're not into that sort of thing, because who hasn't dreamed of screwing Edward Cullen in *Twilight?* Have at it!

5

THINGS

TO DO WHEN

YOU REALLY

SHOULD BE

ASLEEP

Not that this has anything to do
with menstruation, but when
you're lying there, wide-awake and
bored out of your skull at 1:30 a.m.,
this is a really good list to have on hand.

1

PAINT YOUR NAILS IN OMBRE

You'll need two different shades of nail polish, a make-up sponge, and maybe even a YouTube tutorial. I gave myself some ombre nails once and it's not easy, but if it ends up being a mess you can always blame it on the fact that you are too artsy for your own good.

2

PEEL AN ORANGE IN ONE CONTINUOUS PIECE

Start by loosening the peel at either end of the orange, and then peel it in a spiral. You'll have to start again with a new orange if the rind breaks. If you end up peeling all the oranges, you can always turn them into OJ for breakfast.

3

LEARN A NEW SKILL

Like belly rolling, for example, or hitting Top C—
High C (which is a freakishly high note; listen to
Swedish singer Pernilla Wahlgren in "Piccadilly
Circus" at the 2:10 mark on the video). It's amazing
that it's even physically possible, but I have practiced
devotedly over the last four nights.

4

REDECORATE

Dragging heavy furniture across the floor when your
parents/siblings/neighbors are sleeping next door
isn't especially considerate, but you seldom think
things through when the clock indicates that it's way
past your bedtime, while at the same time your brain
insists that your bed absolutely must be on the other
side of the room for a better floor plan. This is sweet
revenge at six in the morning when your neighbor has
practiced High C until 3:00 a.m.

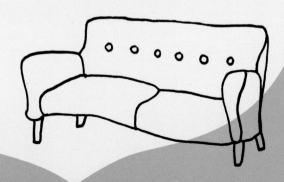

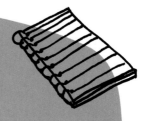

5

WRITE YOUR OWN LIST

Write down five things you or someone else can do when you or they can't sleep. There's an endless number of ways to keep busy during nighttime hours, and these are only five of them. I've provided a few lines here so you can jot them down, because I'm just that generous page space.

EPILOGUE/ THANKS/ SO LONG

THE BODY IS AN
AMAZING

When I decided to write a book about menstruation, the hardest part of the whole project was coming to grips with how little I actually knew about my subject. I thought I had a pretty good understanding of ovaries and estrogen levels, until I noticed that I was spending more time Googling facts than writing about them. Plus, it's crazy how information can differ from one website to another. *The Health Guide* says one thing, Wikipedia claims something else, and then various menstruation-themed homepages have their own slants, which is a clear indication that we have mostly considered menstruation a trifling matter.

I'M NOT AN EXPERT ON MENSTRUATION

I'm not a midwife, either. I've attempted to share the knowledge I have accrued so far, but a lot of the content of this book is made up of opinions that are purely personal, because I don't know all there is to know about menstruation. Also, I have not taken into consideration every possible scenario that could happen when you have your period, because I just don't have explanations for everything. But that's one of the fun things about menstruation!

For instance, a while ago I was trying to figure out why I'd been menstruating every two weeks for the past three months. My period had suddenly become very irregular, and I had no idea why. It was totally spooky. I couldn't imagine where all the blood was coming from, and I was almost driven to tears because not only was I living on my own in an expensive apartment in Stockholm, having to pay for all my food, bills, and rent, I was also buying double the tampons since I was now bleeding twice a month instead of once. I did a Google search,

MYSTERY

and the answer that came up was cancer. That makes for *great* reading for someone like me, who's a bit of a hypochondriac.

Another blood-soaked month passed before I settled back into my old normal, thirty-day cycle. I suppose my body simply decided that I could do with a little extra menstruation for a while. Indeed, this can happen, and it

time to time. Just about anything can happen when you have your period. All hail the power of the period.

THE GYNECOLOGIST IS YOUR FRIEND

However, I did promise my likewise hypochondriac mom to have my double periods checked out, because it sounded like a good plan to me (even if the nurse

It is menstruation's prerogative to have its own way from time to time. Just about anything can happen when you have your period. All hail the power of the period."

is perfectly normal. Being stressed out can disturb your cycle; but it can also just be a small thing that makes your period heavier or lighter for a bit. Once, someone told me in a comment on my blog that she had met a guy whom she liked a lot, and she suddenly started having her period at shorter intervals because her body was gearing up for love and baby-making. It's your period's prerogative to have its own way from

told me that everything was A-OK) and because it's stupid to tempt fate when it comes to these things. If any of you have a weird experience like the one I had, or one weirder still, get on the phone and call your doctor for an appointment, or go to your nearest health clinic. While you're there, you can also ask about things that I didn't cover in this book, and hopefully you'll get a reliable answer.

THANK YOU!

Thanks for reading my period piece—pun intended. I hope you've enjoyed it! I also hope that I will be PMSing when this book is released. Having a book published is great; that the book in question is about menstruation is even better; seeing this little creation, with my own face inside, displayed in bookstores is going to be nothing short of amazing— but imagine the intensity of these feelings if I could experience all this while having PMS, too. There'll be a downpour of tears! My narcissism will know no bounds! Oh, how I hope it'll work out that way!

THANKS, AND BYE!